CISTERCIAN STUDIES SERIES: NUMBER FIFTY-SEVEN

NICOLAS COTHERET'S

ANNALS OF CÎTEAUX

CISTERCIAN STUDIES SERIES: NUMBER FIFTY-SEVEN

NICOLAS COTHERET'S
ANNALS OF CÎTEAUX

Outlined from the French original

By LOUIS J. LEKAI, O.CIST.

CISTERCIAN PUBLICATIONS
KALAMAZOO, MICHIGAN
1982

+ 1997+

Available in Britain and Europe from
A. R. Mowbray & Co. Ltd.
ST THOMAS HOUSE   BECKET STREET
OXFORD OXI ISJ

Library of Congress Cataloguing in Publication Data

Lekai, Louis Julius, 1916-
   Nicholas Cotheret's Annals of Cîteaux.
   Nicolas Cotheret's Annals of Cîteaux.

   (Cistercian studies series; no. 57)
   Includes bibliographical references.
   1. Abbaye de Cîteaux. I. Cotheret, Nicolas, 1680-1753?
Annales de Cisteaux. II. Title. III. Series.
BX2615.C48L44   271'.12'04442   82-4371
ISBN O-87907-857-X   AACR2

Linotyped at Galesburg, Michigan by Francis Edgecombe   *Printed in the United States of America*

TABLE OF CONTENTS

v

PREFACE

The *Annals of Cîteaux* by Nicolas Cotheret is an important but not particularly attractive work of monastic historiography. It is the only known monograph of that great abbey and incorporates a large number of hitherto unknown incidents and many unpublished documents. But as a whole it attracts only professional scholars endowed with a thorough knowledge of early eighteenth century French, of which the author himself was not a great master. The rigid chronology does not help the flow of narrative; neither does the insertion of long documents of varying relevance. But the most disturbing feature of the work is the author's penchant for constant moralizing, for a pessimistic and invariably disparaging analysis of both events and characters, often without sufficient justification.

The present outline is intended to familiarize the reader with the largely unknown factual details and offer a shortened narrative for easy reading and quick reference. The frequent subtitles (not present in the original), the notes, the appendix and index may facilitate the attainment of the same goal.

The author's own words are always between quotation marks. The bulk of the text is mine, although I took great care not to represent ideas or opinions alien to the author's mentality and general purpose. My few critical remarks are restricted to the notes. Incidents of drastic abbreviations are chiefly the omission of documents, irrelevant critical excursions, and long pages of censorious outbursts of indignation.

This modest abridgement is never meant to be a substitute for the original. It is my hope that Cotheret's *Annales de Cisteaux* in a modern edition will soon be at the disposal the scholarly public.

L. J. L.

INTRODUCTION

THE MANUSCRIPT outlined on the following pages lay dormant for two centuries. It was only in 1935 that a Parisian bookseller offered it for sale to Dom Alexis Presse, then abbot of the Trappist monastery of Tamié, an eminent historian and collector of Cistercian manuscripts. He promptly bought the bulky folio, but his subsequent involvement in the revival of the Breton house at Boquen prevented him from the exploitation of his new acquisition.

A few years later the work passed through the hands of another Trappist scholar, J.-M. Canivez, who recognized its importance, although he was not impressed by its general character. Fortunately, though, the *Dictionnaire d'histoire et de géographie écclésiastiques* had not yet passed the letter 'C', so, in 1956, he wrote a paragraph on Nicolas Cotheret and his newly discovered *Annales de Cisteaux* in the thirteenth volume of this monumental reference work. This was the first occasion that the scholarly world had a chance to notice the existence of this curious manuscript.

Somewhat later a third Trappist researcher, Anselme Dimier, discovered that the Municipal Library of Dijon holds two other copies of the same manuscript and in 1960 he added this new information to another paragraph on Cotheret written for the ninth volume of the *Dictionnaire de biographie française*.

For some reason, however, these short references to a new discovery failed to spark the imagination of Cistercian scholars and awareness of the existence of the three volumes did not create a rush for their further examination, which they certainly deserved.

The Manuscripts

All three surviving manuscripts show some distinct characteristics, but none can be identified as the autograph. All carry some notes about the author and the transmission of his work, although in this the scribes or owners who added these notes are not in agreement. Nevertheless, there is no doubt about the author, Nicolas Cotheret, librarian and archivist of Cîteaux, who began his work in 1736.

The two manuscripts of Dijon are closely related: MS 2475 is a copy of MS 2474. The latter is the work of a number of professional scribes, but MS 2475 was made by one hand, that of Louis-Bénigne Baudot (1765-1844) of Dijon, advocate, book-collector, and renowned antiquarian. He completed the task on January 20, 1792, in the belief that he had copied the author's original manuscript. This explains why the title (*Mémoires pour servir à l'histoire de l'abbaye de Cisteaux*) and the text of these two manuscripts are identical, although both have a variety of appendices added to the *Memoires* through the industry of copyists or owners. MS 2474 contains a document about the General Chapter of 1765 (therefore it must have been copied after that date), a chronological list of abbots of Cîteaux and a collection of documents related to the history of Cîteaux that Cotheret had no time or opportunity to incorporate into his narrative. This manuscript has an intriguing feature: above the title there is the name of a certain Chantepinot *puisné*, but neither the identity nor the role of this individual can be determined. Was he one of the scribes or owners of the volume?

The copy made by Baudot, MS 2475, has, in addition to what he found in MS 2474, a detailed table of contents, a short essay on the origins of Cîteaux by Cotheret, and a large variety of odds and ends of more recent origin, including illustrations. But the strangest thing is that Baudot apparently became interested in Cistercian history and kept adding to the original text innumerable marginal notes, corrections, critical remarks and supplemental bibliography, making the whole work appear confused, disorderly, and certainly difficult to read. Furthermore, in 1812 Baudot acquired the Tamié manuscript and discovered that this much larger work had inserted into the text many documents entirely missing from MS 2474 and from his own copy. He therefore copied the missing documents on separate sheets and glued them into his own manuscript between the corresponding pages.

As they are, both Dijon manuscripts have a common drawback: the lines of the writing go to the edge of the sheets, therefore in the process of binding the last words or letters of lines are often covered.

The best preserved and most useful is the folio-sized copy in the possession of the Abbey of Tamié in French Savoy. It is also the work of several hands, but the writing is easily readable and nowhere obstructed. Although the narrative is the same as that of the Dijon copies, it incorporates, as we mentioned above, many documents missing from the other two copies. On the other hand, the documents appended to the Dijon manuscripts are missing from the Tamié copy, although the text constantly refers to this non-existent collection. Moreover, only the Tamié manuscript is introduced by a history of the text of reasonable authenticity. Its title too differs from those of the Dijon copies: it is simply *Annales de Cisteaux*.

The peculiarities of the Tamié volume pose obvious questions which at this time cannot be answered with certainty. The most puzzling is the origin of the unique documents which must go back either to the author or someone closely associated with him. The time of its completion is equally doubtful, although it was certainly finished by 1812. The outline presented here is based on this Tamié manuscript.

The Author and his Work

Toward the end of the seventeenth century the Cotheret family of merchants in Dijon was a large one. Among the baptismal records of Dijon citizens during the period in question, carefully preserved in the Municipal Archives, one may find several individuals bearing the same name: Nicolas Cotheret. There is little doubt, however, that the Cistercian

author of our *Annals* is to be identified with the Nicolas Cotheret who was born on February 7, 1680, and baptized on
the same evening at the collegiate church of Saint-Étienne.
He was the child of the 'honorable Simon Cotheret merchant
of Dijon and the honest Pierette Pignalet his wife'.

Nicolas must have joined the abbey of Cîteaux at an early
age. We have two lists of the membership of the abbey, one
from 1699, the other from 1719 (*Cistercienser-Chronik*, 21
[1909], 178; 9[1897], 246); on the first Cotheret is already
mentioned as a professed monk; on the second, he is designated as librarian and archivist of the abbey. Several of his
early writings, all in manuscript, add after his name the title
of 'doctor of the Sorbonne', but the legitimate use of this
degree is doubtful, since his name is missing from the records
of the theological faculty of the University of Paris. It is very
likely, however, that he spent some years in the College of
Saint Bernard in Paris, for he relates in his narrative an incident about a student in 1702, that he must have witnessed
himself.

For whatever reason, he was recalled from Paris before
his graduation, although his talents were recognized in his
appointment as librarian and archivist. This opportunity
accorded him the time and facilities for research and writing
dedicated to the history of Cîteaux. His early unpublished
studies show no particular distinction, but his reputation as
scholar must have spread beyond his community, for the editors of a new version of the *Gallia Christiana* turned to him
for a reliable list of the abbots of Cîteaux (GC IV[1728],
984, 990).

Meanwhile, he continued his research, aiming at a full history of the abbots of Cîteaux. But as his work progressed,
he became ever more pessimistic, convinced that for all the
calamities of his beloved abbey, responsibility lay with in-
competent, negligent, or tyrannical abbots, against whom
the monks remained forever helpless. Since he never concealed his conviction, he had to work in total secrecy and

hide his highly critical notes from curious eyes. At the time of the election of Abbot General Andoche Pernot in 1727, the royal representative, the Intendant of Dijon, carried a letter of exclusion naming three monks whose candidacy was unacceptable to the royal court. One of them was Cotheret, although he received no vote at all, therefore his name was not published (*Cistercienser-Chronik*, 12[1900], 275).

This incident seems to support two assumptions: that he had acquired the reputation of a potential troublemaker; and that he had no party, no followers, certainly few friends, and was by his strange behavior isolated in the midst of his community.

That Cotheret started working on the final draft of his great manuscript in 1736, he himself tells us (Tamié MS, fol. 72ᵛ). The date of its completion remains uncertain. But certain it must be that his relationship with the new abbot deteriorated to the point that Pernot decided to get rid of him, and in fact obtained for him a *lettre de cachet*. In the last minute Cotheret managed to smuggle out his voluminous manuscript to a confidential friend, Gabriel Pothier, prior of the Benedictine Saint-Vivant, and waited calmly until he was escorted to the place of his exile, the abbey of Bonnevaux, where he died probably in 1753, aged seventy-three.

According to the preface of the Tamié manuscript, after the death of Pothier, Cotheret's work passed to Pothier's scholarly nephew, Jean Belot 'le Cadet', a retired businessman in Dijon. The existence of the manuscript came to the knowledge of Belot's friend, Jean-Baptiste Faux, procurator of the Parlement of Dijon, who, with the permission of Belot, procured a copy of it for his own use. All this happened before Belot's death in 1758.

The autograph was inherited by Belot's brother, Michel, who knew nothing about the nature of the manuscript and presented it as a gift to Cîteaux's last abbot before the Revolution, François Trouvé. According to the author of the preface (perhaps M. Faux himself), when Trouvé realized the true character of the work, he made sure that it would never scandalize posterity by destroying it.

At that moment the only surviving copy of Cotheret's history was the one made at the request of M. Faux; consequently all other copies must be derived from this supposedly faithful proto-copy. The Dijon manuscripts offer other theories about the survival of Cotheret's work, but there is no explanation for the different and unique features of the Tamié manuscript.

By 1812 all presently known copies of the *Annals of Cîteaux* were in the possession of Louis-Bénigne Baudot. His son, Claude-Louis-Henri, an equally famous archaeologist, held together the great collecton of manuscripts and rare books until his death in 1880. After this date the collection was dispersed and the Cotheret manuscripts went into commercial circulation.

Cotheret, the Historian

At a superficial glance Cotheret's work does not reveal its unusual character. Writing the story of a famous abbey, following the pattern established by the great Maurist historians, was very much the vogue early in the eighteenth century. The structure of the work, proceeding by centuries and within them following the sequence of abbots, was a commonplace method of presentation. The large number of inserted documents, the concentration on lawsuits, controversies, and unusual calamities of all sorts fill countless pages in all similar works. Even Cotheret's erudition was no greater than the average of the time. He was well-versed in the readily available works of reference and used the documents in his own archive with considerable skill, but there is no indication that he made efforts in trying to consult libraries or archives other than his own.

What makes the reading of Cotheret's monograph a unique experience is his sharp critical mind and his indomitable courage in pouring out his unhappiness without restraint. This pessimistic attitude toward the past made him alert to mistakes and abuses which he presents with a moral indignation spiced with instructions for posterity.

About the first century, for lack of sources, he has not much to say, but from the thirteenth century on his narrative swells to epic proportions. Some of his preferred topics are in fact monographs within the monograph. Among these are the perennial feuding of the abbots of Cîteaux with the proto-abbots, those of La Ferté, Pontigny, Morimund and specifically Clairvaux; the endless calamities with Gilly and its original owner, the abbey of Saint-Germain-des-Prés of Paris; the attempt of the emerging Strict Observance to capture Cîteaux and with it the rest of the Order; the constant threat of financial disaster, always attributed by Cotheret to reckless spending and inept and wasteful administration.

In vain would the reader search for details of internal community life. Still, some glimpses can be caught on occasions of abbatical elections, or when the author tries to justify his low opinion of practically all abbots from the fourteenth century to his own times. He admits only three exceptions: Jean de Cirey (1476-1501), for his efforts to save the Order from the scourge of the *commenda*, to solve the problem of Gilly, and to keep under control the scheming abbot of Clairvaux; Claude Vaussin (1645-1670), for his victory over the Strict Observance; Jean Petit (1670-1692), for his triumph over the proto-abbots.

The author's prejudices against all who wield authority are so glaring that they are hardly defensible. But he assumes the position of ordinary monks of Cîteaux who have no protection against the abuses of tyrranical superiors. As he repeatedly explains, this is Cîteaux's unique predicament. In other monasteries the abuses of an abbot can always be tempered by father-abbots, visitors, or by intervention of the General Chapter. But who is above the abbot of Cîteaux? That he could ignore even his own council and other constitutional limitations of his power with impunity seems to be a valid observation.

To voice such charges took an unusual degree of courage and sense of responsibility and justice. Cotheret certainly realized that his work could not be published and would bring him calamities if discovered while he lived. His only reason to commit to posterity his observations was the hope that some members of a future generation might use it as an effective arsenal of weaponry in their fight for a more equitable administration of the mother-house of his beloved Order. The radical solution of the French Revolution frustrated all such expectations, but posterity is still enriched by a powerful voice for a renewed monasticism.

MEMOIRS FOR A HISTORY OF
THE ABBEY OF CÎTEAUX

(Fols. 1-1ᵛ)

The Author's Preface

"THE FACT that little effort was given to the preservation of the documents of the past, particularly those of the twelfth and thirteenth centuries, renders impossible the task of presenting a full history of Cîteaux." We, therefore, must restrict our narrative to the calamities of the six centuries of history that prevented the abbey from reaching the status of secure wealth, no matter how persistently was it attempted.

Since the intention of the founders was the establishment of a place of simplicity and love of poverty, it was obvious that God could not bless the worldly efforts of their successors. "Hence the public calamities, bad administration, foolish enterprises, the love of splendor and vanity of abbots, their comfortable and idle life, their absolute and crushing domination, the inexperience, presumption and foolhardiness of their officials, a multitude of litigations of all kinds, one more embarrassing and expensive than the other, and many other miseries which very often led them to the verge of annihilation."

THE FIRST CENTURY
(Fols. 1ᵛ-20)

The Foundation

SAINT ROBERT, after he realized at Molesme that abundance in material things had impoverished the monks in spiritual goods and corrupted their morals, left everything behind and, favoring the hidden and penitential life, departed for the desert of Cîteaux, accompanied by twenty-one monks

1

just as zealous observers of the Rule of Saint Benedict as he himself was.

They arrived at that place of solitude on March 21, 1098, which was in that year not only the feast of Saint Benedict but also Palm Sunday. They were favorably received by Odo I, duke of Burgundy, and Raymond, viscount of Beaune, and Hodierna, his wife, the owners of Cîteaux, who donated the place with its surroundings to the monks. The Duke of Burgundy confirmed the donation and permitted the exploitation of the adjacent forests, together with portions of his own domain.

Shortly thereafter the same duke donated to the monks the vineyard of Meursault which, according to the charter issued by Hugues II, his son, happened on the feast of Christmas. Duke Hugues freed this property from the payment of tithes due to Hugues de Chevigny, who was indemnified by the duke through the annual payment of ten sous. This arrangement was confirmed by Bishop Nargod of Autun,[1] in whose diocese the vineyard was situated.

Saint Robert

The first great trial of the New Monastery was brought about by the jealousy of the monks of Molesme, who attempted through Pope Urban II to force the return of Abbot Robert. The pope entrusted the matter to his legate, the archbishop of Lyon,[2] who succeeded in persuading Robert to return to Molesme after having spent only fifteen months in the New Monastery. The rest of the founders of Cîteaux resented the desertion of Robert so much that for more than a century Robert's successor, Alberic, was considered as the first abbot of Cîteaux.

Although the anonymous biographer of Saint Robert[3] asserts that he himself appointed his successor at Cîteaux, according to the history of the beginnings of Cîteaux,[4] Alberic was canonically elected abbot by his fellow-monks, and this version must be accepted as the authentic one. It was only the General Chapter of 1222 which recognized Saint Robert as the first abbot of Cîteaux, and designated April 17 for the celebration of his feast.[5]

The same biography of Saint Robert is responsible for two other errors: first, asserting that Alberic died two years after his appointment; then adding that even his successor, Stephen Harding, was appointed by Robert who, in fact, retained the administration of both Molesme and Cîteaux. The same *vita* erred even in stating that Saint Robert lived to be ninety-three years old and died on April 17. The editors of the new *Gallia Christiana*[6] (vol. IV, col. 732) contend that he died on March 21, 1110, exactly twelve years after the foundation of Cîteaux, although his feast was eventually transferred to April 29. This was the reason why the Cistercian Breviary, as another deplorable error, asserts that Abbot Robert died on April 29.

Alberic and the Papal Protection

The first resolution of Alberic, the new abbot, was to insure the safety and security of the New Monastery by obtaining a bull of papal protection. With this intention he sent two of his monks to Pope Paschal II. His envoys carried letters of recommendation from Cardinals John and Benedict, who were active in France in the matter of the divorce of King Philippe I from Bertha of Holland, his wife; from Gauthier, bishop of Chalon; and from Archbishop Hugues of Lyon. The mission was successful and the monks returned with the requested bull, dated April 18, 1100, taking Cîteaux under papal protection against any further vexation.

It would be highly desirable to have the original copy of the bull, for the surviving copies do not contain identical texts. The version incorporated into an ancient collection of manuscripts shows that Paschal II confirmed Cîteaux conditionally, i.e., until the monastery lived according to the rules and intentions of the founders.[7] The same conditional phrase can be read in the first printed copy of the bull, edited by

Abbot Jean de Cirey in 1493.[8] The same conditional version
was adopted by Henriquez in his *Menologium Cisterciense*
(Antwerp, 1630), and by two editions of the *Magnum Bullarium Romanum* (Rome [1638], p. 52, and Lyon [1692],
I:56).

On the other hand, the conditional phrase is missing from
a copy of the *Exordium Cistercii*,[9] which is in the library of
Cîteaux, and in another copy toward the end of two ancient
Martyrologia in manuscript. The same text is featured at the
head of the *Bibliotheca Cisterciensis* (Bonnefontaine, 1660)[10]
and in the *Nomasticon Cisterciense* (Paris, 1664).[11]

Which of the two versions is the authentic one?[12]

One might be inclined to give the preference to the text
incorporated in the *Exordium Parvum*, lacking the conditional phrase, and reprinted as such in the *Bibliotheca Cisterciensis* and *Nomasticon Cisterciense*. In these cases, however, the key verb, *roboramus*, is obviously misplaced in the
context, since this word belongs to the omitted conditional
phrase. This renders the text of the bull featured in the
Exordium Parvum suspicious.

No suspicion can be justified concerning the text reprinted
by Jean de Cirey and the *Magnum Bullarium Romanum*,
rendering the text in its integrity.

When was the conditional phrase suppressed in the text
of the *Exordium Parvum?*

One may only answer that the copy of this narrative preserved in Cîteaux and bound together with the above mentioned *Martyrologia*, is of thirteenth century origin, an
epoch when the fervor of the first founders had already become a thing of the past. It may be possible that at that time
the retention of the conditional phrase referring to the initial
observance of Cîteaux had become a source of embarrassment and potentially dangerous, should someone challenge
the validity of papal protection and the subsequent privileges the Order of Cîteaux had enjoyed. Without these the
Cistercians would have no alternative but surrender to epis-

copal jurisdiction. The avoidance of this eventuality might have motivated the deletion of the momentous but dangerous phrase. Subsequent papal bulls of protection from Alexander III to Alexander VII never intended to abrogate the condition set by Paschal II.

Stephen Harding

Stephen Harding, an Englishman who succeeded Alberic, had been serving at Cîteaux as prior and belonged to the founders of the house. He added to the regulations of his predecessor rules that excluded the use of gold, silver, silk, and similar costly materials from liturgical usage and emphasized the importance of solitude by refusing hospitality to the duke of Burgundy, who was used to holding his court at Cîteaux.

In spite of such uncompromising attitude, the abbey was enriched under his administration by goods granted by the abbeys of Saint-Germain in Paris, Saint-Benigne of Dijon, Saint-Jean-d'Angély, the seigneurs of Vergy and many other eminent ecclesiastics or lay persons.

Saint Bernard and the Expansion

Abbot Stephen's greatest consolation was the arrival of Saint Bernard with his thirty companions. This made possible in rapid succession the foundations of La Ferté, Pontigny, Clairvaux and Morimund, the first four daughters of Cîteaux. It was this growth in membership that necessitated the publication of the Charter of Charity, composed by Abbot Stephen himself, a document full of wisdom and piety. During the rest of his administration Cîteaux became the mother of more than eighty foundations.

The multiplication of personnel and territorial expansion justified the request addressed to Pope Innocent II that he confirm all possessions of Cîteaux. It was granted without delay, dated at Cluny on February 10, 1132. The same pope granted to the whole Order exemption from the payment of

tithes as long as the monks themselves cultivated their own
lands and cared for their own animals. The same bull exempted Cistercians from attending diocesan synods, except
when matters of faith were at stake.

Problems Following Stephen's Resignation

Shortly thereafter Abbot Stephen, afflicted by the various
disabilities of old age, resigned from his position. His successor was Guy (Wido), whose conduct did not, however,
please him; therefore he was removed and replaced by Raynald, son of Milon, count of Bar-sur-Seine, and a monk of
Clairvaux.

The year of Stephen's resignation is uncertain. The Spaniard Manrique asserts in his *Annales*[13] that the date was 1133,
without offering any proof. We are equally ignorant about
the reasons of Guy's removal or the length of his administration. Manrique, following the *Exordium Magnum* of Conrad
of Eberbach,[14] says that he was deposed with the concur-
rence of the General Chapter for some unspecified 'bad conduct', after only a few months of his election.

Robert of Mont-Saint-Michel in his treatise[15] on the changing condition of monastic orders (fol. 811), assures us that
Guy, abbot of Trois-Fontaines, was elected under the pressure of Stephen himself, but Guy abandoned his office foolishly, after having served as abbot of Cîteaux for two years.

Which of the two opinions is the correct one?

It is certain that Robert was abbot of Mont-Saint-Michel
in 1154, and therefore a contemporary witness, noted for his
credibility. Conrad, on the other hand, abbot of the far-away
Eberbach, wrote almost a century after the events described,
dying in 1227.

As to the date of Saint Stephen's death, we read in his
legend that he died on March 28, 1134. Therefore if we sup-
pose that Robert of Saint-Michel was correct in saying that
Guy governed Cîteaux for two years, we must assume that

Saint Stephen resigned a few days after the issuance of the above-mentioned bull of Innocent II.

Meanwhile the Order was growing so fast that in 1152, according to the testimony of Robert of Saint-Michel, it already possessed five hundred abbeys. This was the reason why Abbot Goswin, successor of Raynald, at the General Chapter of the same year, when Saint Bernard was still alive, prohibited the initiation of new foundations.[16]

The goods of Cîteaux multiplied in proportion. They were enumerated in a confirmative bull of Alexander III in 1164. It is remarkable though that nothing was mentioned about tithes, seigniories, or purchases of properties.[17]

But in this world of ours blessings never come unmixed.

Cîteaux and Alexander III

In about the same year (1164) the same Alexander III ordered the abbot of Cîteaux to depose the abbot of Clairvaux. The brief to this effect is in the great collection of Dom Martène (vol. II, p. 706) of the Congregation of Saint-Maur, who found it in a manuscript in the abbey of Saint-Vaast in Arras, entitled *Registrum Epistolarum Alexandri P.P. III.* The brief is neither dated nor does it name the abbot of Cîteaux.[18] It is known, however, that it was issued in Sens, where the pope arrived in October 1163, and remained until the feast of Easter, 1165. Accordingly, the abbot of Cîteaux was Gilbert, successor of Fastrède, who had died in Paris on April 21, 1163, and to whom the pope had administered the last sacraments in the presence of the king. It was the same Gilbert who presided over the General Chapter attended by King Louis VII, imploring the monks to pray for the birth of an heir and successor. His son, named Philippe (Augustus) was born on August 22, 1165. This incident is told by Fleury in his *Histoire ecclésiastique*, vol. XV, book 71.[19]

The reason the pope demanded the resignation of Abbot Geoffrey of Clairvaux (previously abbot of Igny and secretary of Saint Bernard) was that he 'displeased Henry, arch-bishop of Reims, and brother of King Louis VII'. The pope argued that the reputation of one of the most illustrious houses of the Order was at stake; therefore he entrusted the investigation of the matter to the same archbishop of Reims, the bishop of Auxerres, and the abbot of Cîteaux. The last was to persuade Geoffrey that the wisest course would be his quiet resignation. In case of resistance, the abbot of Cîteaux was to depose Geoffrey and proceed with the election of his successor.

It is unknown with what resolution Gilbert pursued his delicate mission; we know only that he died before he could complete it. According to the annalist of the Order (Man-rique), his death occurred in 1166, although we know that he was alive in 1167, since in that year he signed a contract with the canons of Autun.

It was only in 1168 that Gilbert's successor at Cîteaux, Abbot Alexander, deposed the recalcitrant Geoffrey, who defended himself ably before both the General Chapter and the Roman authorities. Meanwhile Pope Alexander III not only remained inflexible, but also issued a bull on July 4, 1169, addressed to Alexander of Cîteaux, in which he pro-hibited any appeal in cases when an abbot was facing depo-sition for public scandal, or after having been found guilty of crimes. Under such circumstances Geoffrey was forced to leave Clairvaux, although his place of retirement remains unknown.[20]

Cîteaux and Saint-Benigne of Dijon

In 1171 Cîteaux began to experience that it was impossible to accumulate earthly goods and still enjoy the tranquillity of monastic life. The community received from the duke of Burgundy the house which had once belonged to Duchess Mathilda, wife of Hugues II, son of the founder of Cîteaux. The building was in Dijon, close to the river Ouche, below the walls of the abbey of Saint-Benigne. The abbot of this

Benedictine community complained about this transaction, whereupon the duke promised to pay to Saint-Benigne annually and in perpetuity ten sous as a recognition of the feudal rights of the abbey over the house and its surroundings. The contract was never executed in this form, although Cîteaux still claimed the property. Saint-Benigne protested, but the case was decided by the arbitration of an ecclesiastical committee composed of Guichard, archbishop of Lyon and legate of the Holy See, Gauthier de Bourgogne, bishop of Langres and son of the donor of the property, and Pierre, bishop of Chalon. They decided that the house and its surroundings should remain in the possession of Cîteaux, but that the conditions burdening the Cistercians were onerous. They were to pay annually and in perpetuity forty sous to Saint-Benigne; they were prohibited ever to build a church on the location or to use it for a cemetery, mill, fulling mill, tan-house or oven, and even fishing rights were denied to the new owners. They were permitted to use the water, however, or even divert it directly to or around the house. Attempts by Cîteaux to modify this highly restrictive agreement will be told below.

The Famine of 1177

In 1177 a great famine afflicted the country. One may read in the chronicle of Guillaume de Nangis[21] that although the monks of Cîteaux themselves suffered much, they sold the treasures of their church in order to feed the starving poor. Manrique in his *Annals of Cîteaux* mentions the same incident (vol. I, p. 473) referring to the *Chronicle of Auxerre*, which praises for his extraordinary generosity Abbot Guillaume I of Cîteaux, who set aside a definite portion of his abbey's revenues for the poor.

It was in the same year that Geoffrey, the deposed abbot of Clairvaux, was elected abbot of Haute-Combe in Savoy, while Henry, his predecessor at Haute-Combe, became abbot of Clairvaux. Geoffrey dedicated to Henry his fourth book of commentaries on the Canticle of Canticles, which is among the manuscripts of Cîteaux.

The Canonization of Saint Peter of Tarentaise

Five years later (1182), the General Chapter decided to initiate steps for the canonization of Peter, archbishop of Tarentaise,[22] originally a monk of Bonnevaux in Dauphiné and later abbot of Tamié in Savoy. Accordingly, a deputation was sent to Rome, made up of the abbot of Bellevaux and our Geoffrey of Haute-Combe. The pope, Lucius III, however, before anything else, demanded the composition of a reliable *vita* of the archbishop. Pierre, abbot of Cîteaux (who became bishop of Arras), together with the abbot of Clairvaux, entrusted the task to Geoffrey, who accepted the commission. His letter to this effect, together with two others, are at the head of the *vita*, bound between Saint Bernard and Saint Malachy in a folio volume preserved in the library of Cîteaux.

In the same year (1182) the same pope, Lucius III, issued a brief in confirmation of all goods and possessions of Cîteaux (Beaune, Meursault, Crépey, Gergueil, Rosey, Vaugeot, Moisey and Toutenant), which, though considerable, still did not include purchases, tithes, or seigniories.[23]

The Consecration of the Church of Cîteaux

It is remarkable, though, that the church of Cîteaux had not yet been completed, and it was in the same condition as late as 1188, for in that year Gerald de Montsaugun, doyen of Langres, donated a vineyard in the village of Couchey for the completion of the church. Finally, it was consecrated on October 17, 1193, by Robert, bishop of Chalon, under Abbot Guy Paré, who was created cardinal bishop of Preneste in 1202 by Innocent III, and took the see of Reims in 1203. The church of Cîteaux served as the burial place of the ducal family of Burgundy.

On the occasion of the dedication of the church it was open also for women. But urged by the abbots of La Ferté, Pontigny, Clairvaux and others, Abbot Guy Paré prolonged this favor by three days, during which time nuns chanted the Holy Office together with the monks. The General Chapter of 1194, indignant over this unusual and illegal procedure, rebuked those responsible for it and ordered that the donations collected during those three days be taken away and spent by the proto-abbots according to their best judgement.[24]

The Beginnings of Gilly

According to the testimony of the first volume of the ancient chartulary of Cîteaux, during the administration of Saint Stephen the monks received, for a modest annual compensation, a piece of land from the abbey of Saint-Germain of Paris. Late successors of this saintly abbot sought to expand this property by the acquisition of additional land belonging to the nearby priory of Gilly, a dependency of Saint-Germain. A treaty to this effect was negotiated under the auspices of Peter, cardinal bishop of Tusculum. Accordingly, Cîteaux was to pay to Gilly for the new acquisition the customary tithes in the form of nine setiers[25] of grain, half wheat, half oats. In the meantime, however, Cîteaux promised not to reach out for other lands attached to Gilly without the prior consent of Saint-Germain.

When was this treaty signed?

Certainly during the time when Cardinal Peter was active in France. Leaning on the authority of Alfonso Chacon,[26] Fernando Ughelli,[27] Mézeray[28] and Moreri,[29] one may conclude that the most likely date was 1199, during the abbacy of Robert IV of Saint-Germain (1192-1202). The subsequent violation of this contract by Cîteaux brought only misfortune to the greedy community.

THE SECOND CENTURY
(Fols. 21-42ᵛ)

Illegal Acquisitions

THE MONKS OF CÎTEAUX no longer adhered to the early restrictions concerning acquisitions of property or to the prohibition of accepting tithes and seigniories. Thus, before he joined the Fourth Crusade, Guillaume de Chanlite, viscount of Dijon, in 1202 donated to Cîteaux for candles and other necessities of the church, twenty setiers of wheat and ten setiers of fodder, financed from the tithes collected at Ouges. The same act exempted the monks from the tithes attached to the vineyards of Brochon.

In 1205 Cîteaux was involved in a feud with the abbey of Maizières, which accepted for burial a son of the duke of Burgundy, while Cîteaux claimed the exclusive privilege of the bodies of the ducal house. In fact, the General Chapter of 1205 decided the case in favor of Cîteaux and placed Maizières under interdict until the duke's delivery to Cîteaux.[30]

Somewhat later Cîteaux refused to pay for the vineyard in Dijon tithes due to the abbey of Saint-Benigne, under pretext that the Order was tax-exempt. After much negotiation, on February 26, 1208, Abbot Adam of Saint-Benigne signed an agreement with Cîteaux. Accordingly, for the payment of two hundred livres of Franche-Comté, Cîteaux was freed from any further payment for properties within the seignorial domain of Saint-Benigne.

In the following year Duke Odo III of Burgundy donated to Cîteaux a portion of his forest in Fez (Faux), and permitted the monks to gather wood in other parts of his forests or use the same as pasture for their animals. In 1212 the same duke transferred to Cîteaux free of any charge his seigniory known as Corcelles-le-Bois, together with all rights and privileges connected with the possession, except the right of 'high justice', i.e., inflicting capital punishment, which he retained for himself and his successors.

Furthermore, the duke permitted the monks to alter the flow of the river Saulon so that it was diverted by means of an aqueduct through the territory of Noiron. This gesture helped not only the monks but the duke himself, as he often held his court at Cîteaux, where he had an apartment separated from the monastic enclosure. But the execution of the project was costly to Cîteaux, because all those who had been affected by the detour of the river had to be indemnified. The duke proved to be helpful even in such matters. In 1214 he issued a charter obliging himself and his successors to come to the aid of the monks, if in the future claims would be raised against Cîteaux in matters of water-rights. This happened in the case of the canons of Langres, who received as compensation the annual rent of ten livres, and the inhabitants of Noiron, who were granted the use of the duke's forests.

In 1216, Odo, lord of Chaulx, sold Cîteaux a portion of tithes he owned in Corcelles-le-Bois; the same contract was approved by the duke of Burgundy. In 1218, Hugues-de-la-Corvée and his wife donated to Cîteaux the annual income of ten setiers, half in wheat, half in oats, which belonged to them in the village of Ouges.

Taxes and the Secular Clergy

About this time the Order was molested by avaricious pastors in certain provinces, who opposed the entry of their parishioners into a Cistercian abbey unless they received the fee due to them for a funeral. When this practice came to the knowledge of Pope Honorius III, in a bull issued on June 7, 1221, he condemned such abusive practices and insured the free profession of Cistercian novices.

A worse problem was caused by the aggressive collectors of ecclesiastical taxes, who went beyond the original intent of the decision passed by the Fourth Lateran Council (1215) under Innocent III, in support of Cistercian tax-exemptions. In order to settle the issue once and for all, on November 9, 1224, Honorius III issued a bull which exempted from taxation not only possessions of the Order held in 1215, but later acquisitions as well, if they were cultivated by the monks or by others at the expense of the monks. Another bull of the same year, dated November 25, extended the same privilege to lands once alienated but later repossessed by Cistercians.

Troublesome possessions

The growing livestock of Cîteaux, raised for profit, prompted successive acquisitions of land. According to a contract of 1225, the monks purchased the seigniory of Ouges from Odo de la Marche, son of Guillaume de Chanlite, for the sum of 1000 marks of silver. The agreement was, however, soon contested. In the following year Guillaume de Vergy, lord of Mirabeau and grand seneschal of Burgundy, claimed rights over the property as a kin of the vendor, although he was forced to renounce his supposed rights under the pressure of Hugues de Montréal, bishop of Langres, and Alaïde de Vergy, duchess of Burgundy. It was the same Duchess Alaïde, who in 1231 prevailed upon Guillaume de Chanlite, brother of the vendor, to abandon his claims against the monks, after he received from them sixty livres of Dijon.

In 1232, Aimon d'Aiserey, provost of Saint-Jean-de-Losne, donated to Cîteaux half the tithes collected at Brasey and some months later half of those from Montot. The monks meanwhile obliged themselves to furnish annually and in perpetuity for the benefit of the Sainte-Chapelle of Dijon ten heminas (about thirty liters) of grain, half wheat, half oats.

The greed of the abbey could not go unpunished by God, and the decline of Cîteaux, both material and moral, became obvious in the next few years, culminating in 1238 in the excommunication and deposition of Abbot Jacques I.

The Misfortune of Abbot Guillaume and His Company

His successor, Guillaume III de Montagu, monk of Clairvaux, experienced further troubles of a different nature. As he traveled by sea in the company of several other abbots (Clairvaux and l'Epau) for the general council in Rome convoked by Gregory IX in 1240, the ship was captured by Henry, king of Sardinia and illegitimate son of Emperor Frederick II. The abbots were held for three years. Abbot Guillaume of Clairvaux died in captivity and it was only through the intervention of King Louis IX of France that the others were released in 1243. The abbot of Cîteaux resigned and retired to Clairvaux, where he died shortly afterwards.

The Visit of Louis IX

Matthew Paris, English Benedictine,[31] reports in his *Annales* (p. 439) that on September 29, 1244, as the abbots of the Order convened at Cîteaux for the annual General Chapter, King Saint Louis of France arrived together with his whole court for a visit.[32] As they approached the abbey, they all reverently dismounted. At the gate they were received by five hundred abbots coming out to the illustrious guests in procession. On this occasion the king's mother, Blanche of Castile, received permission from the pope to enter the enclosure of the abbey in the company of twelve of her ladies in waiting. This was the king's first visit at Cîteaux.

According to the same historian, Pope Innocent IV wrote a letter to the same General Chapter and implored the monks to intercede on his behalf before the king, asking him to grant the pontiff asylum in France and to save him from the persecution of Emperor Frederick. The monks did so, falling on their knees before the king, who was so deeply moved that, kneeling with the monks, he promised to do his best for the safety of the pope.

It was on this occasion that the General Chapter, as a special favor, permitted meat to be served to the royal guests, who occupied the apartments of the dukes of Burgundy. The Chapter pointed out, however, that the papal permission granting women the favor of entering monastic enclosures, did not entitle the guests to be accommodated overnight within the enclosure.

In grateful memory of the royal visit the Chapter granted their majesties a number of spiritual favors, among them anniversary masses in perpetuity for their souls by every priest of the Order.

Stephen Lexington and the College of Saint Bernard

The successor of Abbot Guillaume of Clairvaux was an Englishman, Stephen Lexington.[33] He was greatly embarrassed over the fact that Franciscans and Dominicans received higher education, while Cistercians did not. He, therefore, turned to Pope Innocent IV, who permitted him to organize a college in Paris for his own monks. The novel institution, however, was much criticised within the Order, since the permission was obtained without the previous knowledge of the General Chapter. On the other hand, any action against the move could be interpreted as an affront to papal authority. In fact, at least indirectly, the college was recognized by the Chapter in 1248, 1251 and 1254.[34] Still, Manrique in his *Annales* asserts that Abbot Guy III of Cîteaux used the incident as a pretext for the deposition of the abbot of Clairvaux in 1256.

The college survived, nevertheless, and the General Chapter decreed that the title of its superior should be provisor, and that students from other houses, at home or abroad, might attend it, although all should remain under the jurisdiction of the abbot of Clairvaux. Among other regulations, the Chapter of 1254 permitted the admission of novices in the belief that the institution might attract many vocations among the young scholars of the city.

The deposition of the abbot of Clairvaux as his punishment for the illegal establishment of the college remains debatable. It is true that the fact of the deposition was referred to as late as 1681 by Abbot Jean Petit as a proof of his superior authority over the College of Saint Bernard, contested by the proto-abbots. It is also true that under the portrait of Stephen Lexington preserved at Clairvaux it is clearly stated that he was deposed by the abbot of Cîteaux. But one may justly ask, if the statutes of the General Chapter in behalf of the College passed before the deposition, could they not be taken as approvals of the institution? If so, what was the justification of the deposition, which is nowhere mentioned in the acts of the Chapter?

The *Annales* of Matthew Paris throw a revealing light on the problem (pp. 631, 643). He asserts that among the enemies of Stephen Lexington the rumor was spreading that he had obtained a brief from his patron, Pope Alexander IV, which stated that the abbot was irremovable in his see at Clairvaux, and that this groundless suspicion was the motive behind his actual deposition. The indignant pope not only denied the existence of the brief, but demanded the restoration of the abbot at Clairvaux and the due punishment of his detractors.

At this point King Louis IX intervened in Rome, arguing that the authority of the General Chapter must be upheld at any cost, and finally convinced the pope that the act of deposition must be executed. The same source insinuates that this was achieved after Cîteaux had bribed the Roman officials by the distribution of a large sum of money. A resolution of the General Chapter of 1257, ordering the payment of an unspecified "grand affair", seems to substantiate this possibility.

The subject of so cruel and groundless a persecution bore his trial with exemplary humility and spent his last years in exile. He never lost the confidence and friendship of Alexander IV who, shortly before Stephen's death, offered him an episcopal see in England (Manrique, *Annales*, I, 510).

Finally, one may call attention to the curious fact that the opposition to the College was based on the allegation that it was initiated without the previous permission of the Chapter, and not on the obvious breach of the century-old law prohibiting Cistercian foundations in cities.

The General Chapter of 1260, in order to prevent accidents in the distribution of Holy Communion under both species, decreed that with the exception of the servers at the altar, all others should receive only the host.[35]

The Feud Between Cîteaux and Clairvaux[36]

In 1262, the monks of Clairvaux elected for their abbot Philippe I, monk of Foucarmont and originally canon of the cathedral of Mans, a man well versed in legal matters. When in the same year Urban IV created Guy, abbot of Cîteaux, cardinal of Saint Laurence in Lucina, the monks of Cîteaux elected as his successor Jacques II, their former prior, without, however, inviting the four proto-abbots for the occasion as the Charter of Charity demanded. This inexplicable incident furnished an opportunity to Philippe of Clairvaux for avenging the defeat of his predecessor and launching an unprecedented attack against Cîteaux.

The combat began at the General Chapter of 1263, when the new abbot of Cîteaux rejected one of Philippe's nominees for definitor. The abbot of Clairvaux decided to appeal to Rome. Urban IV tried to disarm the belligerent Philippe by offering him the episcopal see of Saint-Malo. He, however, not only declined the promotion, but also proceeded to see the pope in Rome. Abbot Jacques countered the move by prohibiting the journey and ordering Philippe to appear before him under pain of excommunication. Since the abbot of Clairvaux was already on his way to Rome, Jacques commissioned Béralde, abbot of Maizières, to intercept him, force him to turn back and make him promise to accept the proffered bishopric. Bérald overtook Philippe on January 6 in Villeneuve on Lake Lausanne, but his mission was entirely fruitless. Philippe continued his journey to Rome, where he obtained a papal audience and was so successful that the pope withdrew his appointment to Saint-Malo.

The abbot of Clairvaux exploited his opportunity to the fullest. He disclosed the irregular circumstances of the election of his adversary, complained about the indignities he had had to suffer at the previous General Chapter, and characterized the conditions at Cîteaux and throughout the Order in such dark colors that the pope became convinced of the necessity of a thorough reform. To investigate the charges, therefore, he on March 15, 1264, appointed a commission composed of the bishop of Troyes,[37] the abbot of Marmoutier,[38] and Geoffrey,[39] Dominican confessor of King Louis IX.

The finding of abuses was no difficult task. It was true that the last election at Cîteaux had been held without the prescribed formalities. It was equally true that the regular visitations of Cîteaux by the four proto-abbots had been inconsequential formalities; that the General Chapter no longer fulfilled its original purpose, passed useless and contradictory statutes and intimidated upright and conscientious abbots; that the abusive acts of the abbot of Cîteaux remained unpunished; that the visitations of abbeys had become an oppressive financial burden on the houses visited, while the visitors often behaved in a scandalous manner and interfered with the free election of abbots; that some of the ablest abbots were being forced to resign; that the abbots of Cîteaux terrorized their subjects by undeserved excommunications, while they themselves often seized the abbatical seals in times of vacancies in abbeys under their jurisdiction and used them for frivolous purposes.

Meanwhile Philippe of Clairvaux was busy in organizing his party in order to influence the outcome of the investigation of the papal committee. To all the abbeys of the filiation he sent a circular letter, which was answered by a declaration in his support signed by his faithful adherents.

The abbot of Cîteaux counter-attacked on April 29, 1264, by ordering the abbot of Clairvaux to appear before him within two weeks. Philippe, however, was not found in his abbey, whereupon Abbot Jacques attempted to take control of Clairvaux under the pretext of a canonical visitation. But the monks of Clairvaux, obviously well-instructed, denied entrance to him. The irate Abbot of Cîteaux countered the move by the excommunication of all officials of Clairvaux and placed the whole abbey under interdict.

Abbot Philippe fired back by charging that he was unable to comply with the demand of the abbot of Cîteaux, and he was not to be deterred by threats from following the course he had taken for the reform of the Order. In a letter addressed to the bishop of Langres[40] he asked for protection against Cîteaux. The bishop promptly complied, and on May 16, 1264, warned the abbot of Cîteaux under the pain of excomunication to abstain from any drastic action during the course of an investigation conducted by the papal commission. Indeed, on May 18, the commission invited all parties concerned to attend a consultation scheduled for July 23 in the city of Langres.

Meanwhile, King Louis IX, who apparently had little confidence in the success of the papal delegates, decided to take the matter into his own hands. He ordered the contestants to appear before him, demanding that both lift their mutual excommunications. For the investigation of the conduct of the officials of Clairvaux he appointed a royal commission.

On June 9, the pope sent a brief to Cîteaux and ordered the abbot to cease any action against Clairvaux and to cooperate with the papal committee. Abbot Philippe, in fear for his personal safety and for his party, on July 2 obtained another papal brief which permitted him and his adherents to abstain from attending the General Chapter or other meetings until the current process of investigation was completed.

Both abbots, surrounded by their respective supporters, appeared before the papal committee in Langres, but the abbot of Cîteaux merely declared his intention of appealing from the committee to Rome and, in fact, departed for Italy the same evening. He gave as his reason the boycott of the General Chapter by Clairvaux. Abbot Philippe, too, made preparations for still another trip to Rome. The members of the papal committee, general confusion notwithstanding, sent their report to Rome.

One may find the full documentation of this "grand affair" in the *Nomasticon Cisterciense* (pp. 375-464), although the individual items are not chronologically arranged. According to a manuscript entitled *Dialogus prioris et subprioris* by an anonymous author,[41] Philippe was motivated more by jealousy than by the desire for reform; his party never included the abbots of La Ferté and Pontigny.

Any action toward the resolution of the pending issues was temporarily suspended by the death of Urban IV on October 20, 1264. His successor, Clement IV, was elected on February 5, 1265.

The new pope was just as anxious to restore peace among Cistercians as his predecessor. He issued a general absolution of both parties from any ecclesiastical censures they might have incurred, coupled with an invitation to all leading abbots of the Order to work out in his presence a solution of all pending issues.

The result of such consultations was the apostolic constitution *Parvus fons*, issued on June 9, 1265. It recognized the validity of the last abbatical election in Cîteaux, although for the future insisting on the validity of the old custom, namely the presence of the four proto-abbots, without, however, granting them active vote in the election. The elected abbot of Cîteaux was to be considered the legitimate superior even before his confirmation by the Holy See. The document specified the procedure for selecting the definitors and prescribed the annual visitation of Cîteaux by the proto-abbots, although their rights consisted only in reverential exhortations. In order to reduce the expenses of canonical visitations, the visiting abbot was to come with no more than ten horses; visitors of lower rank were restricted to six horses. The deposition of abbots was limited to the gravest abuses.

The Indebtedness of Cîteaux

Cîteaux came out of the conflict heavily indebted. Clement IV, sympathetic with the plight of the abbey, on March 5, 1267, appointed the abbot of Saint-Germain of Auxerre to assess the financial condition of Cîteaux. His findings were depressing. The abbey owed to a number of creditors the total of 20,000 *livres tournois*. The pope then issued a warning to the creditors not to harass the abbey, but to wait until each could be paid by Cîteaux. On the other hand, the abbey was obliged to liquidate the debt by setting aside annually 4,000 *livres* for the purpose. The same brief urged the General Chapter to come to the aid of the hard-pressed mother-house.

Since neither the creditors nor the General Chapter took seriously the pleading of the pope, on December 15 of the same year Clement IV addressed an energetic order to the General Chapter to make an organized effort for the collection of contributions on Cîteaux's behalf. The Chapter of 1268 evaded action by referring to the extraordinary taxes the Order was forced to pay to the royal government under the pretext of launching a new crusade. It was only in 1269 that the Chapter came up with a proposal, feeble as it was. It authorized the abbot of Cîteaux to exempt twenty foreign abbots from attending the Chapters of 1270 and 1271, and collect from them their travel expenses, using the sum for the liquidation of still outstanding debts.[42]

Improvements and New Purchases

Conditions must have improved under the administration

of Jean I, successor of Abbot Jacques, for in 1282 he was able to purchase for 3,200 *livres tournois* properties in the seigniory of Chaugey, Maison-Dieu and the faubourg of l'Ône, held previously by the brothers Philippe and Jean de Vienne, sons of Hugues, count of Vienne. If one may believe the authors of the new *Gallia Christiana*, Jean I, formerly abbot of Savigny, who as such had had a significant role in the upheaval created by Philippe of Clairvaux, not only paid off the debts and acquired the above properties, but built around Cîteaux a brick wall which was more extensive than the present one.

The same ameliorating conditions prevailed until the end of the century. In 1298 Abbot Ruffin, through the co-operation of Robert II, duke of Burgundy, on June 26 obtained a bull from Boniface VIII by which the pope authorized the abbot to confirm in his name the election of the doyen of the Sainte-Chapelle of Dijon, if the election was uncontested. This favor saved this modest benefice the expenses of a Roman confirmation.

Abbot Ruffin died on November 30, 1299, and his successor, Jean de Pontoise, formerly abbot of Igny, began his administration by paying, still in the same year, 1,500 *livres* to the monks of Saint-Germain of Paris in relief of the mortgage burdening Gilly, a priory near Cîteaux, but dependent on Saint-Germain.

THE THIRD CENTURY
(Fols. 43-70)

The Acquisition of Gilly

THE CONFUSED AFFAIRS of the abbey of Saint-Germain of Paris, suffering under the weight of exorbitant debts, forced the monks to find ways for easing their burdens. The most obvious move seemed to be the unloading of the priory of Gilly by offering it for sale to its immediate neighbor, Cîteaux. The monks turned with the problem to Boniface VIII in a letter dated March 10, 1300, telling the pope that they had been unable to administer effectively the distant Gilly, exposed to the spoliation of rapacious neighbors. Therefore they asked the pope to grant permission for selling Gilly to the Cistercians. They proposed a purchase price to be paid immediately, and a reasonable annual rent to be paid by Cîteaux in perpetuity.

In the same month Cîteaux offered Saint-Germain the sum of 5,000 *livres petits tournois* for Gilly, together with all its dependencies and revenues, the money to be paid as soon as the legal formalities could be arranged through the provost of the Châtelet of Paris.

Gilly was a considerable benefice, donated to the monks of Saint-Germain in 1044 by Robert I, duke of Burgundy, brother of King Henry I. It possessed the tithes of the villages of Gilly, Chambolle, and Morey, together with the lands, seigniory, and tithes of the town of Bichot.

Momentarily, however, the financial status of Cîteaux was threatened by the extortionary scheme of Duke Robert II of Burgundy, who unexpectedly contested Cîteaux's right to exercise "high" and "low" justice within its own domain. It was useless to prove that the abbey had possessed such rights from its foundation. The duke needed money and he threatened to revoke the monks' judicial privileges unless they paid him 11,000 *livres*. The hapless Cîteaux had no choice but to pay, whereupon the duke generously insured the contested rights to the abbey "in perpetuity". But this was not the end of vexations. On the eve of the following Easter the duke forced the monks to swear allegiance to him as their overlord before Henry, archbishop of Lyon, and the act placed Cîteaux under his guardianship and protection, of dubious value.

Boniface VIII, yielding to the request of Saint-Germain, issued a bull on September 28, 1300, which united the priory of Gilly with Cîteaux, on the condition that the Cistercians keep in the priory three monks in perpetuity, insuring the continuation of religious services; that they pay in one sum 10,000 *livres petits tournois* to Saint-Germain, in addition to an annual rent of 400 *livres petits tournois* to be paid on the feast of Assumption, until Cîteaux could find and buy for Saint-Germain a property of the same rental value near Paris.

The details of the actual transfer of Gilly to Cîteaux were entrusted by the pope to the abbot of Saint-Étienne of Dijon, the abbot of Oigny, and the doyen of the collegiate church of Beaune. The final ceremony took place on December 2, when Brother Guy, grand cellarer of Cîteaux, in the name of his abbot, promised to fulfill the stipulated conditions and obligations; thereupon he received the key of the church of Gilly.

On the part of Saint-Germain in Paris the formalities of transfer took place on February 22, 1301, marred by the dissenting voices of seven monks who intended to appeal against the deal to the pope. Within a week, however, they were prevailed upon to change their minds; thus the final act could be completed on February 27, including the signing of a receipt for the 10,000 *livres*. On March 9, all vassals and tax-paying subjects of Gilly were ordered to change their allegiance and pay all their dues to Cîteaux.

Finally, one must remark that Cîteaux remitted the 7,000 *livres* previously advanced to Saint-Germain, attested to by the above mentioned documents of December 12, 1299 and March 11, 1300, on condition that, should the monks of Saint-Germain in future interfere with the quiet possession of Gilly, Cîteaux would have the right to reclaim the original loan of 7,000 *livres*. Thus Cîteaux paid for Gilly, in fact, 17,000 *livres*, not counting the annual rent of 400 *livres*.

Dom Bouillard of Saint-Germain[43] in his book entitled *Histoire de l'abbaye de Saint-Germain-des Prés* (p. 145) deplores the loss of Gilly and asserts that the reason for the pope's prompt action in favor of Cîteaux was that he himself had been a Cistercian and that the abbot of Saint-Germain spent in the papal curia 1,400 gold florins and 400 *petits tour-*

nois. The truth remains, however, that the transaction was initiated and promoted by Saint-Germain, and that Boniface VIII had never been a Cistercian.

The manuscript history of Saint-Germain by Dom Dubreuil[44] (fol. 121ᵛ) goes even further, insisting that prior to his election as pope, Boniface had been abbot of Cîteaux. The same error emerges in a decree of the Parlement of Paris in the fifteenth century, issued in behalf of Saint-Germain. The material foundation of this error might be the fact that there was an abbot of Cîteaux in the middle of the thirteenth century named Boniface (1244-1255), who, however, died in 1258, shortly after his resignation.

The Calamities of Cîteaux under Jean de Pontoise

While some monks of Saint-Germain felt cheated by the alienation of Gilly, the acquisition brought no happiness to Cîteaux either. One may even single out this event as the beginning of the decadence of Cîteaux. The same abbot, Jean de Pointoise, who proudly took credit for the enrichment of Cîteaux, was destined within three years to watch helplessly the devastation of his abbey, brought about by his own imprudence.

King Philippe le Bel, engaged in constant feuding with Boniface VIII, in the month of June 1303, convoked the three estates to Paris in order to seek support for his appeal against the pope to a future council. While all participants supported the king, Jean de Pontoise refused to sign the declaration against the pope. This was his way to express his gratitude toward the pontiff not only for Gilly, but for a bull issued on December 18, 1301, by which all properties of the Order, of whatever nature or condition, both present and future, were exempted from ecclesiastical taxation.

It is true that some historians, such as Dupuy[45] and later Baillet,[46] in his *Histoire des démêléz de Boniface VIII avec Philippe le Bel* (p. 195), assert that the signature of Jean de

Pontoise was on the document of June 13, 1303. But this is an error. In fact, the same Baillet (p. 341) reports that Boniface, on the day he was taken prisoner, expressed his gratitude for the courage of the abbot of Cîteaux, who alone sided with him in the dispute. That it was only the abbot of Cîteaux who refused to sign the royal declaration can be read in the chronicle of Guillaume de Nangis and in Mézeray's *Histoire de France* (vol. II, p. 330). Had Jean de Pontoise signed the declaration, the subsequent pillage of Cîteaux by royal troops could not be explained.

The devastation is described in a manuscript (fol. 7ᵛ) bearing the title: *Relation véritable de tout ce qui a été fait pour se libérer entièrement envers l'abbaye de Saint-Germain-des-Prés de la rente de 400 petits tournois que Cîteaux luy devoit annuellement à cause du prieuré de Gilly.*[47] A royal army thoroughly devastated Cîteaux and all its dependencies. The soldiers took from the granges 14,000 sheep, uncounted numbers of horses and other domestic animals, and carried away from Cîteaux simply everything movable, leaving the monks in such misery that its effects could be felt until the end of the fifteenth century. Many other abbeys of the Order in France had to bear similar consequences of the king's wrath.

Jean de Pontoise, according to the testimony of the Dominican chronicler, Nicolas Trivet, in order to allay the king's ire, resigned from his abbacy. The continuator of the chronicle of Nangis confirms the same, adding that the resignation took place in 1304.

The exact date of the resignation, however, cannot be determined. Fragments of the epitaph of Jean de Pontoise reveal that he was abbot for three and a half years. As we know that Ruffin, his predecessor, died on November 30, 1299, he must have resigned a few days after his fateful resolve not to sign the royal declaration against Boniface VIII. The same epitaph gives for the date of his death March 25, without, however, marking the year.

The new abbot of Cîteaux, Henry, formerly abbot of Jouy, managed to regain the good will of the king, who in June 1304 issued a patent of royal protection for the Order in France. In it he admitted the damage caused by his troops and hinted at some aid for reconstruction, but there is no evidence of effective help.

Cîteaux, Avignon and Gilly

At the request of Abbot Henry, on December 1, 1309, the new pope in Avignon, Clement V, united the priory of Gilly with the parish of the same locality; the union was to take effect after the death or resignation of the pastor then in charge. The change took place in 1314, when the pastor, Pierre de la Chapelle, resigned, and Pierre de Dijon, Cistercian prior of Gilly, presented to Elie, bishop of Autun, as curate Guillaume Guibaudet de Flagey. He was accepted by the bishop and received for his services annually 50 *livres tournois*.

The same Abbot Henry represented the Order at the Council of Vienne convoked by Clement V in 1311.

Clairvaux and the Sale of the Parisian College

In 1320, the financially overburdened abbey of Clairvaux, unable to maintain the College of Saint Bernard in Paris, offered the institution to the whole Order. With the consent of Abbot Guillaume of Cîteaux and the General Chapter, the transfer was effected on September 14, 1320, by a contract which included a monetary compensation to Clairvaux.

The College was in deplorable condition. In spite of its annual revenue of 16,000 *livres* in rents, it was deeply in debt, largely because of a lack of students and the insufficiency of tuitions paid for each student by his own abbey. The morale of the students was low, the discipline lax, so that the doctors and other graduates of the College scarcely helped halt the general decline of the Order.

Problems at Gilly

Since the isolated condition of the three monks who lived in Gilly in fulfillment of the bull of union created frequent disciplinary problems, Abbot Guillaume turned to Pope Jean XXII for help in finding an effective remedy. The understanding pontiff on December 1, 1328, issued a bull which permitted Cîteaux to withdraw the monks from Gilly and replace them with three secular priests whose position was to be dependent on Cîteaux. This bull, however, was never executed.

The Reform of Benedict XII

There is no doubt that the proximity of the papal court in Avignon presented a temptation to the abbots of Cîteaux to ask and receive privileges and prerogatives contrary to the ancient regulations of the Order. The reversal of this trend was the intention of the Apostolic Constitution of July 12, 1335,[48] issued by the successor of Jean XXII, Benedict XII, who was elected on December 20, 1334.

Pope Benedict had entered the Cistercian Order at Boulbonne (diocese of Mirepoix) and later become abbot of Fontfroide (diocese of Narbonne), therefore he had an intimate knowledge of the problems that afflicted his Order. As soon as he took charge of his high office, he began work on the reform of the Cistercians, taking into his council the abbots of Cîteaux, La Ferté, Clairvaux, and Morimond.

Since he was convinced that the root of all evils was the despotic and often inept administration of abbots, particularly in financial matters, his reform aimed at the curbing of abbatial powers by granting greater influence to the council of monks representing the whole community. The key member was to be the bursar, the chief fiscal officer, to whom all others who handled money were expected to give an account.

In order to eliminate the useless and showy equipage of abbots he reduced the number of horses for the proto-abbots to six, for others to four. Interestingly, the same pope chose not to tamper with the privileges of the abbot of Cîteaux, who remained free to use as many carriages or horses as he pleased.

Another significant portion of this Consttiution dealt with the reorganization of higher education, particularly the administration of the College of Saint Bernard in Paris. He initiated from his own funds the construction of a still missing church on the campus, the cornerstone of which was laid on May 24, 1337, by Jeanne de Bourgogne, wife of King Philippe de Valois, son of Robert, duke of Burgundy, and Agnes de France, daughter of Saint Louis. Unfortunately, this good pope died too early to see the completion of the ambitious project, and the avarice of subsequent Cistercian generations left the church unfinished.

The Enfeeblement of the 'Benedictina'

On February 12, 1337, Guillaume IV, abbot of Cîteaux, died, and his place was taken by Jean de Chaudenay. He was the first abbot of Cîteaux who had to pay to Avignon 300 florins for the confirmation of his new position, an amount which was to be raised considerably in the future.

The abbots, who could never be reconciled with the curbing of their authority, saw their opportunity after the election of Clement VI on May 7, 1342. The abbot of Cîteaux wasted no time. After only a few days of negotiation in Avignon, he obtained from the new pope on October 7, 1342, a bull which removed from the Constitution of Benedict XII the canonical punishments of abbots found delinquent in the execution of its terms. This encouraged the abbots to resume their absolute rule over their monasteries without the danger of facing unpleasant consequences. The flow of the costliest Burgundian wines from Cîteaux to Avignon facilitated further concessions in favor of abbots, whose power could not be controlled by the General Chapter simply because that assembly turned out to be a convention of fellow-delinquents.

The Plague and Its Consequences

The bubonic plague, which in these years afflicted the country, resulted in the desertion of many abbeys of the Order. Grasping neighbors exploited their opportunities and seized much of the unguarded monastic properties. Jean de Rougemont, successor of Jean de Chaudenay of Cîteaux, turned for help to Clement VI, who in 1351 appointed guardians (*conservateurs*) for the endangered communities, individuals who, for due material compensation, volunteered to safeguard monastic patrimonies. The remedy, however, proved worse than the disease. These men, often called administrators or stewards, once appointed, could no longer be dislodged, although they worked more for their own enrichment than for the benefit of the monks. This was the beginning of the eventually institutionalized *commendators*, who within a century eliminated most regular abbots in France and endangered monasticism itself. This is how God punished the pride, ostentatious wealth, and tyranny of abbots.

Jean de Rougemont died on May 27, 1359, and was succeeded by Jean de Buxières who, like his predecessors, had to pay 300 florins for his papal confirmation.

Litigation with Saint-Germain-des-Prés

By 1360 the value of traditional monetary units had changed so considerably that the new abbot insisted on the re-negotiation of the payment of 400 *livres petits tournois* due annually to Saint-Germain for the possession of Gilly. Claiming uncertainties in the matter, Cîteaux refused to pay anything in 1360, 1361, and 1362. The inevitable litigation ended in February 1363 with the decision that the 400 *livres* should be counted as *livres tournois*, fixed to the value of a silver mark (=4.5 *livres tournois*). At the same time Cîteaux was obliged to pay at once the arrears of 1,200 *livres*. Cîteaux refused to accept the verdict as the last word in the dispute. This was only the beginning of over a century of litigation, the expenses of which surpassed by far the revenues collected from Gilly.

The Pope and the Wines of Cîteaux

Pope Urban V was well informed about the sufferings of monastic establishments due to the Hundred Years' War and the periodic recurrence of the plague. As a gesture of good will toward Cîteaux, he issued on April 1, 1364, a bull in which he strictly prohibited any further shipment of wine as Cîteaux's gift to Avignon, either for himself or for anybody else in the papal curia. The customary quantity of wine must have been very considerable, since disobedience to the bull was to be punished by excommunication. That such gifts had been used as bribes serving the interest of the abbots of Cîteaux is also understood from the tone of the bull.

The Fortification of Gilly

The continued war between France and England and the threat of roaming bands of undisciplined mercenaries justified the efforts of Jean de Buxières to fortify the church and conventual buildings of Gilly, where the valuables of Cîteaux and even those of the neighboring population could be kept in safety.

For the execution of the project the permissions of the bishop and the duke of Burgundy were necessary. Bishop Godefroy of Autun granted his consent on October 12, 1367, and a day later Duke Philippe le Hardy, also concurred with the request.

When the abbot realized the magnitude of the undertaking and the formidable expenses it involved, he turned again for help to Duke Philippe, who on February 18, 1368, ordered the governor of the bailiwick of Dijon to furnish the necessary material assistance. The completion of the difficult undertaking not only increased the respect for the abbot of Cîteaux, but also induced Duke Philippe to appoint Jean de Buxières as his councilor, the first such title granted to any abbot of Cîteaux.

Pope Gregory XI and Cîteaux

Urban V, who died on December 19, 1370, was succeeded on the 30th of the same month by Gregory XI. Just as happened after Benedict XII, the new pope revoked the bull of his predecessor prohibiting the gifts of wine furnished by Cîteaux. As we learn from the new[49] *Gallia Christiana* (vol. IV, col. 1001), Jean de Buxières did not hesitate to exploit his opportunity; he sent to the pope 30 *bottles* (each about 600 liters) of wine to Avignon, partly from Beaune, partly from Gevrey. Gregory XI expressed his thanks in a letter of May 2, 1372, adding that he would find ways to prove his gratitude for the generous gift. He made good his promise on December 20, 1375, when he granted Abbot Jean the cardinal's hat under the title of Saint Laurence of Lucina. But the new cardinal could not enjoy his dignity for long; he died at Avignon on September 4, 1376.

His successor at Cîteaux was Gérard de Buxières, probably a nephew of his predecessor, and formerly abbot of Fontenet. According to a manuscript entitled *Declaratio liberationis Cistercii erga Sanctum Germanum,*[50] his end was tragic: he hurried to Paris carrying a large sum of money, ostensibly in order to settle the perpetual feud with Saint-Germain over Gilly, but in fact he wanted to become a cardinal. As he approached the city he fell from his horse and died *fractis cervicibus.*

Cîteaux and the Great Western Schism

Abbot Gérard's administration coincided with the beginning of the schism caused by the simultaneous elections of Urban VI in Rome and Clement VII, who chose to remain in Avignon. The latter was generous to Cistercians. On

March 10, 1380, he granted that the abbot of Cîteaux might wear episcopal vestments, and the same privilege was soon extended to Étienne de Foigny, abbot of Clairvaux. Gérard was also successful in purchasing the domain of Rolanges, within the parish of Gilly, for the payment of 110 gold francs in addition to a stretch of land of 7 *livrées* (i.e., netting the income of 7 *livres*) in the territory of Gerlans.

Abbot Gérard, who died on July 9, 1389, was followed by Jacques de Flagny. According to some notes of unknown origin, the tax he had to pay for his confirmation in Avignon was exorbitant: 1,000 francs for the pope and 150 florins for the cardinals, sums entirely disproportionate to the revenues of Cîteaux. One should also bear in mind that according to the 'Clementina' (*Parvus fons*), a legitimate election was considered valid without confirmation by higher authorities. Unfortunately, Cîteaux's wealth was habitually overestimated in the papal curia; therefore such fees kept climbing ever after.

Fire at Gilly

On July 12, 1393, the fortified church of Gilly caught fire and the spreading flames destroyed much of the priory. The conflagration was blamed on the carelessness of the cellarer, Pierre de Troïe, a monk of Cîteaux. His apartment was next to the church and it was there that the fire started in the midst of a boisterous celebration on the eve of the feast of the Translation of Saint Benedict. When all was over, only the refectory remained intact, and was used thenceforth as a wine cellar.

Since the valuable possessions of the inhabitants of Gilly, Vougeot, and Chambolle were kept for safety's sake in the church, where all was destroyed, those who incurred the losses turned to the Parlement of Burgundy, then at Beaune, and demanded that the court force Cîteaux to pay them for the perished articles an indemnity amounting to 6,000 *livres*.

THE FOURTH CENTURY
(Fols. 71-139ᵛ)

As THE AFFLICTION caused by the war and brigandage did not abate in the new century, the monks of Cîteaux turned again to Philippe de Hardy, duke of Burgundy, asking him for permission to fortify the external walls of the abbey. The favor was granted on February 23, 1400. Although in the absence of contemporary descriptions the exact condition of Cîteaux cannot be established, it is obvious that in 1400 most conventual buildings were in deplorable shape.

Another Feud Between Cîteaux and Clairvaux

After the death of Jacques de Flagny in 1405 the monks of Cîteaux elected the abbot of Clairvaux, Jean de Martigny, while the see of Clairvaux was taken by Mathieu Pillard, originally a monk of Des Dunes in Flanders. The agitation was caused by a pamphlet produced by the new abbot of Clairvaux, entitled *Speculum elevationis et exaltationis Ordinis Cisterciensis et etiam finalis depressionis et enervationis eiusdem.*[51] The author asserted, among other absurdities, that during the administration of the first three abbots Cîteaux, together with the first foundations, had been under episcopal jurisdiction until the confirmation of the Charter of Charity by Callixtus II, and that the General Chapter had no legislative power until the same date (1119). One may agree with the *Annales* of Manrique, which insists that the ultimate motive of the work was the undermining of the authority of Cîteaux and the exaltation of the position of Clairvaux.

Cîteaux and the Reform-Councils

The abbots of Cîteaux participated in the efforts to solve the schism between the popes of Rome and Avignon. Jean de Martigny represented the Order with dignity in Pisa (1409) and later in Constance (1414-18). The records of these councils were preserved in the library of Cîteaux. The expenses of the councils and the papal curia weighed heavily on the Church. Cîteaux contributed the assessed amounts, but protested successfully against the separate taxation of Gilly, proving that it was merely a dependent possession of Cîteaux.

After the election of Martin V in 1417, Jean de Martigny sought his protection against the excessive zeal of ecclesiastical tax-collectors. The eventual result was the bull of September 23, 1423, which confirmed once again the Order's tax-exemption, covering Cistercian possessions either cultivated by the monks themselves, or cultivated by others at Cîteaux's expense.

Cîteaux's friendly relation with Martin V encouraged Jean de Martigny to turn to the pontiff with the problem of the annual rent paid for Gilly. The abbot argued that deteriorated economic conditions and particularly the destruction of Gilly left Cîteaux with greatly diminished income, therefore the rent of 400 *livres* was no longer justified, adding that the abbey had been in fact in default of payment for several years. On June 27, 1427, the pope appointed the bishops of Autun[52] and Chalon[53] for the investigation of the case. The results of the inquiry are not known, but it is doubtful that papal authority in a purely economic matter could have prevailed over the royal courts already engaged in deciding the issue.

The Ducal Guardianship

Even more vexing was the problem that Cîteaux had to face after the death of Jean de Martigny on December 21, 1428. The bailiff of Dijon, under the pretext that in the name of the duke of Burgundy he was the guardian of the abbey during the vacancy, sent to Cîteaux his lieutenant, Gérard Vion, who promptly sealed the doors of the abbatial apartment and began to inventory all the goods of the abbey. The greatly disturbed monks first considered an appeal to the Parlement of Paris, but in fear of the duke, Philippe le Bon, they withdrew the appeal and turned with their complaints directly to the duke of Burgundy. He, however, on September 22, 1429, merely transferred the case to the Chamber of Accounts of Dijon. There the monks of Cîteaux had ample opportunity to air their grievances, although the emergency passed with the election of the new abbot, Jean Picart.

Jean Picart and the Council of Basel

Abbot Jean must have been a man of universal respect, for he was delegated to the Council of Basel (1431) not only by his Order, but also as a representative of Duke Philippe of Burgundy and a deputy of the University of Paris. In fact, most of his term as abbot was spent in these and other public duties, so that in 1438 he complained that he had been able to spend only a third of the previous ten years in his own abbey. Although in Basel he played significant roles in various capacities, his stay at the Council was expensive. In 1436 he complained that he had spent 330 gold ducats, whereupon the Council decided to find a way to reimburse him for his expenses. There are no records, however, in proof that the move was fruitful. It is possible though that his taste for Burgundian wines added to the costs of his stay in Basel. At one occasion a large shipment of wine from Cîteaux was held up at Saint-Jean-de-Lône and the authorities forced the Cistercian brothers to pay duties for the transport. An appeal to the duke of Burgundy, however, resulted in the patent of May 6, 1437, which reaffirmed the tax-exemptions of Cîteaux.

Meanwhile the perennial feud over the rent for Gilly continued. Cîteaux insisted on the adjustment of the sum of 400 *livres* to the existing fiscal conditions, and turned for help to Pope Eugene IV. The pontiff replied in a bull on April 16, 1436, declaring the actual value of the *petit tournois* only that of a gold florin. But papal authority in such matters was simply ignored both by Saint-Germain and the Parisian courts, where the litigation continued.

For a while Jean Picart managed to extricate himself from his conciliar duties and attended the General Chapter of 1437, where it was decided, following the instructions of the Council, that Holy Communion should be restricted to the distribution of the host alone.[54]

In 1438 the tension between Eugene IV and the Council fathers in Basel prompted the pope to transfer the sessions to Ferrara, whereupon the opposition in Basel decided on the deposition of Eugene to be followed by a new papal election. In order to escape embarrassing involvement on either side, Abbot Jean decided to leave Basel for Cîteaux. His request for permission to do so was supported by a long memorandum listing his various and urgent duties at home, impressive enough to obtain the needed consent.

Unfortunately, Burgundy did not prove to be very hospitable. On approaching his abbey, Jean Picart and his escort were kidnapped by a gang of notorious highwaymen. The abbot lost not only all his money and other valuables, but was held for ransom for six weeks. The news of the scandalous event disturbed even the busy Council, which appointed the archbishops of Bourges[55] and Auch[56] together with the bishop of Autun[57] to take energetic measures, including the excommunication of all involved malefactors. Later documents are silent about the outcome of the affair.

The Poverty of Cîteaux

Jean Picart died on March 30, 1440, and until his successor was elected, Cîteaux was again exposed to the vexations of the bailiff of Dijon and his officials swarming over Cîteaux under the pretext of guarding its property. After the election of the new abbot, Jean Vyon, the feud with Saint-Germain flared up with new intensity. The Parisian monks rejected the revaluation of the *petit tournois* as suggested by

Eugene IV in 1436, whereupon Cîteaux turned to the same pope once more for assistance. This time Eugene, on December 14, 1443, addressed a letter to the Parlement of Paris proposing that if the monks of Saint-Germain were unhappy with his previous decision, they might return the original 10,000 *livres* to Cîteaux and repossess Gilly. This papal intervention was as much ignored as the previous one and Cîteaux remained under pressure to pay the annual rent as before.

Strangely, although Cîteaux was obviously in financial difficulties, the greed of Jean Vyon was as insatiable as that of his predecessors. On July 23, 1449, he purchased from Jean de Saulx, lord of Meix, a domain near Gilly for the total of 4,125 *livres tournois*. Since the abbot had only 1,600 *livres* on hand, he paid the balance by selling a large number of silver and gold objects he found in Cîteaux, weighing altogether 315 marks and 3 ounces, evaluated at 2,525 *livres*. The list of these objects included many items of liturgical use, such as chalices and patens. But the saddest aspect of this transaction was the fact that Cîteaux was considered to be such a poor risk in financial circles that the abbey was unable to obtain the relatively small loan of 2,500 *livres*. Had the original 'Benedictina' been observed, such a glaring example of maladministration could not have occurred. But in the given circumstances even the General Chapter chose to ignore the scandal.

Meanwhile Cîteaux had accumulated so much debt by the non-payment of the annual 400 *livres* to Saint-Germain that on January 24, 1452, the Parlement of Paris intervened in behalf of the Benedictines, and Cîteaux was ordered the payment of 1,400 *écus* in gold within three years, in addition to the annual rent of 400 *livres*. This time Abbot Vyon turned for support to Pope Nicolas V, who appointed the abbot of Saint-Étienne of Dijon, the doyen of the Sainte-Chapelle of Dijon, and the doyen of Autun as special commissaries in charge of the investigation. In 1453 they attempted to arrange a meeting of the contestants, which, however, never took place.

New Excesses of the Bailiff of Dijon

The General Chapter of 1455 witnessed an unprecedented move of the bailiff of Dijon, who under the same pretext of "guardianship", virtually occupied Cîteaux for the whole duration of the Chapter. The exasperated abbots decided to transfer permanently their conventions to Clairvaux, which was outside of the jurisdiction of the duke of Burgundy. The abuse of these magistrates had grown truly intolerable. They swarmed over the abbey in large numbers, both laymen and their armed escorts, accompanied by as many as fifty horses, so that their support amounted to one-third of the costs of the Chapter. The undisciplined soldiers terrorized the servants of the abbey and threatened them with imprisonment if they did not comply promptly with their extravagant demands.

As a last attempt to avoid the convention's escape to Clairvaux, the Chapter of 1455 turned to Duke Philippe de Bon, who in his patent of July 28, 1456, admitted the abuses and limited the activities of the bailiff of Dijon to a tolerable degree, so that the transfer of the Chapter to Clairvaux never materialized.

New Attempts to Solve the Problems of Gilly

Jean Vyon made another effort to solve the perennial question of Gilly, this time with the help of Callixtus III. In 1457 the pope commissioned the abbots of Sainte-Geneviève and Saint-Magliore, both of Paris, to work out an amicable solution acceptable to both parties. Their efforts were stopped by the death of Jean Vyon on November 25, 1458.

The short administration of his successor, Guy d'Autun, monk of Fontenet and later abbot of Chaalis, was complicated by the ambitious schemes of a favorite of the duke of Burgundy, Jean Joffroy, bishop of Arras, whose great aspiration was to become a cardinal. In order to stay in the limelight, he obtained fror Callixtus III the commission for the general visitation of the Cistercian Order. Although late in 1458 the intervention of the Order's Roman procurator resulted in the revocation of the appointment, there remained the problem of negotiation with the abbot of Saint-Germain. Since all parties admitted that the value of the original *petit tournois* had risen considerably, Cîteaux was to pay 400 *livres* of Paris in addition to an accumulated arrears of the annual rents amounting to 6,000 *livres*.

After the death of Guy d'Autun on July 22, 1462, the monks of Cîteaux elected Himbert Martin. The new abbot realized that the quiet possession of Gilly demanded a radical solution. Accordingly, he obtained from King Louis XI, still in the same year, a patent which authorized the abbot of Cîteaux to purchase a property near Paris of 400 *livres* annual revenue in rent and offer it to Saint-Germain, thus redeeming Cîteaux from this payment forever. Pope Pius II supported the same idea, but the monks of Saint-Germain took an entirely negative attitude.

After this rebuff Himbert turned again to Louis XI, who on August 6, 1466 agreed to a new approach: since Cîteaux received annually from various royal domains 500 *livres* of rent, this sum was to be transferred to Saint-Germain in exchange for the 400 *livres* due from Cîteaux. Himbert hoped that the bait of 100 *livres* in excess would be sufficient to entice the Parisian monks to accept the arrangement, but Saint-Germain distrusted the royal treasury and this offer was rejected as well.

The possession of Gilly created many problems for entirely different reasons. From the early 1460s a close neighbor of Gilly, Guillaume de Vienne, lord of Montbis, initiated a number of lawsuits against Cîteaux, some fought as far away as the Parlement of Paris. Since the reason for the vexations was the fact that the possessions of the lord were intertwined with those of Cîteaux, Abbot Himbert decided to purchase the nobleman's properties and thus consolidate in one block all that the monks possessed around Gilly, including the small château called Le Montbis, east of the priory of Gilly. With the financial and moral support of Claude de Montagu, a descendant of the ducal house of Burgundy, the abbot succeeded. On January 30, 1469, a contract was signed which transferred the disputed territories to Cîteaux for the sum of 9,120 *livres*. Only the future showed the unwisdom of this substantial investment.

Illegal Election at La Ferté

In 1470 the energetic abbot of Cîteaux intervened in the affairs of La Ferté, following the death of Abbot Jean de Saint-Pierre. Namely, the monks of La Ferté, without the knowledge of Abbot Himbert, instead of holding a regular election decided to postulate as their new abbot a Black Monk, Jean de Toulouse, a procedure totally against the Charter of Charity. The indignant abbot of Cîteaux declared the act null and void and, using his authority as father-abbot, appointed to the vacant see of La Ferté Claude de Dinteville, formerly abbot of Rigny in the diocese of Auxerre. The subsequent General Chapter approved and sanctioned the arrangement made by Abbot Himbert.

War and Division of Burgundy

It was about this time that the war between King Louis XI and Charles (le Téméraire), duke of Burgundy, began, and Cîteaux, in the heart of Burgundy, found itself in a precarious position. In order to be prepared for the worst, the monks packed their most valuable papers, documents, gold and silver objects into eight crates and shipped them for safety to the church of Sainte-Madeleine of Besançon.

The war affected even Cîteaux's relationship with Saint-Germain, in so far as Duke Charles prevented the payment of rents to the Parisian abbey, whereupon Louis XI stopped the payment of 500 *livres* to Cîteaux. Charles wishing to compensate Cîteaux and please the abbot (a native of Saint-

Jean-de-Lône), on April 7, 1472, transferred to Cîteaux for a nominal annual rent his small château in Saint-Jean-de-Lône.

The Problem of Abbeys in Commendam

A danger, more menacing than wars, was the increasing frequency of granting abbeys *in commendam* by the Holy See. Under Pope Paul II (1464-1471) a number of Cistercian abbeys, especially in France and Italy, were granted to non-cistercian ecclesiastics, often to cardinals. Paul's successor, Sixtus IV, who was once a Franciscan friar (Cordelier), seemed to be better disposed toward the monks, although he proved to be a man lacking firm resolution. This was most obvious in France, where Louis XI habitually and with impunity rewarded his courtiers and faithful supporters with abbatical titles and revenues.

Abbot Himbert's Delegation to Rome

In order to dramatize the plight of the Order, the General Chapter of 1473 decided to send to Rome a high-level delegation,[58] headed by Abbot Himbert himself, accompanied by the abbots of Clairvaux, Altenberg (Germany), Poblet (Spain) and Jean de Cirey, a native of Dijon, then monk at La Charité and doctor of theology of the University of Paris (ranking first among monks) and soon-to-be abbot of Theuley, representing Burgundy. The same Chapter authorized the collection of 6,000 *livres* to cover the inevitable expenses. By 1474 only half the sum was contributed, which forced the delegation to borrow the missing 3,000 *livres*.

The delegation departed on May 5, 1475,[59] although Abbot Himbert was accompanied only by Jean de Cirey; the others found excuses in the dangers of wars. They arrived at Rome on June 12, and began to work for an early audience with the pope by distributing large amounts of money and gifts to cardinals and other influential members of the curia, among them the cardinals of Bologna,[60] the protector of the Order.

When the day of audience arrived, Himbert poured out all his complaints, begging the pope for his immediate intervention. At the end of his eloquent speech he presented to the pontiff an ornate cup with 1,000 gold ducats in it. According to Dom Cirey, the pope was moved to tears and promised everything the delegates were hoping for. But the conversion of promises to effective bulls and privileges was painfully slow. It was only by mid-September that the documents were ready for publication. Then, however, at a session of the consistory the cardinals raised so many objections that the intimidated pope withdrew the bulls, already signed and sealed.

The Rising Star of Jean de Cirey

In the hope of better luck in the future, the delegation lingered around Rome. In this discouraging situation even the procurator of the Order, the Spaniard Falco Fier, abbot of Saint Bernard of Valencia, turned against the abbot of Cîteaux and secretly co-operated with his enemies. Worst of all, Dom Himbert fell seriously ill and was in this condition when early in February (1476) he was received at another papal audience. Because of Himbert's weakness, Abbot Cirey began to speak with such eloquence and persuasion that the pope appointed him abbot of Balerne, granted a number of indulgences, and re-issued the much hoped-for bulls. But Himbert Martin could no longer enjoy the success: he died on the vigil of the feast of the Annunciation. His faithful companion, the new abbot of Balerne, buried him in the abbey of Saint Sebastian, then a Cistercian establishment. At this very moment the perfidious procurator stole all the valuables from the room of the dead abbot, including his seals, money, and other valuable items. These amounted to a considerable quantity, for Abbot Himbert carried not only the 6,000 *livres*, but all the precious objects he could find in Cîteaux. Tragically, it was not only the

Spanish procurator general, but also Dom Himbert's secretary and almoner who helped themselves to the spoils.

After the burial of Abbot Himbert, Sixtus IV held a consistory, declared the vacancy of the see of Cîteaux and appointed by papal provision Jean de Cirey as the head of the Order. The abbot of Balerne was greatly reluctant to accept the papal favor and suggested instead the appointment of Pierre de Virey, abbot of Clairvaux. The pontiff agreed, and Jean de Cirey himself carried the papal document to France.

The news of the death of Himbert Martin traveled faster than Jean de Cirey. Much before the latter arrived in France, the monks of Cîteaux, knowing nothing about the papal provision, elected as their new abbot none other than Jean de Cirey.

It was only toward the end of April, 1476, that Dom Cirey reached Dijon, where he was received by a delegation of monks from Cîteaux, who told him that they would rather leave their abbey than serve under the abbot of Clairvaux. When Pierre de Virey realized that he would have no chance to govern Cîteaux, he retreated to Clairvaux, while the reluctant Cirey turned to Rome for a bull recognizing the validity of his previous election at Cîteaux. The sinister machinations of the procurator general only delayed action in the matter, but the final result was never in doubt: Cirey received his bull and took full charge of Cîteaux, an impoverished and long-neglected abbey.

The Administration of Jean de Cirey

After a thorough study of the status of Cîteaux, the new abbot decided that the most urgent need was a settlement with Saint-Germain over Gilly. The heart of the matter was the 400 *livres* of rent which, because of the changes of monetary policy, had grown in fact to 1,000 *livres* in actual value.

Immediate action was suspended during the tense months following the death of Duke Charles of Burgundy on January 5, 1476, when the future of the whole Burgundian inheritance became a bone of contention. The western part of the province accepted Louis XI with some reluctance. In Beaune a rebellion was quelled only after a formal siege in 1478, which resulted in the destruction of the house owned by Cîteaux, one of the finest buildings of the town, evaluated at 15,000 *livres*.

In September of the same year Abbot Cirey, who was one of the first of those who had taken the oath of fidelity to Louis XI, was invited to attend an assembly of the French clergy in Orléans. He worked effectively for a compromise between the king and Sixtus IV, while doing his best to stop the spread of the *commendam*. His prominent role assured him a place of distinction among the prelates. It was only with the administration of the city of Beaune that the abbot had to fight. The magistrates of the town could not forgive him his role in winning Burgundy for the king, and afflicted Cîteaux with exorbitant taxes for the properties the abbey possessed within Beaune. Cirey, however, defended successfully the exempt status of Cistercians before a newly established royal court in Dijon.

Losses in Franche-Comté

Less successful was Cîteaux in Franche-Comté which, through the division of the inheritance of Charles of Burgundy, came under Habsburg control. The house of Cîteaux in Dole was burned down, and after its rebuilding it was rented to the magistrates of the town for the purpose of maintaining a grammar school in it. But it was only an ephemeral experiment and the same building was rented for 30 *livres* to Henry Colin, a councillor of the Parlement of Dole. In 1602, Cîteaux sold the house to the town, which in turn granted it to the Jesuits for the foundation of a new college.

The revenues of Cîteaux drawn from other properties in Dole, Besançon, and Léon-le-Saulnier were confiscated by the new government, but the most painful loss was that of

1,100 *livres* of salt revenues from Salins. The treasures of Cîteaux deposited for the sake of safety in the church of Sainte-Madelaine of Besançon turned out to be an even costlier loss for the abbey. During the disorders of the war a treasure-hunting mob penetrated the sacristy of the church and carried away whatever was worth taking from the eight crates.

Toward a Solution of the Problem of Gilly

With all these problems burdening his mind, Abbot Cirey sought the support of the king, whom he found, on his way back from Orléans, in the château of Plessis-du-Parc. His Majesty was most obliging: he ordered the cancellation of the claims of Beaune; authorized the suspension of paying rents to Saint-Germain for five years; and in a patent dated November of 1478, he remitted the 24 *livres* annual rent due for the château in Saint-Jean-de-Lône.

From Plessis-du-Parc the abbot hurried to Paris, where he consulted some of the best lawyers of the city in order to find a way for the liquidation of the rent Cîteaux owed for Gilly. He also sought the advice of two of his confrères, Vincent de Châlon, abbot of Preuilly, and Nicolas de Semur, provisor of the College of Saint Bernard. Unfortunately, both turned out to be entirely unworthy of his confidence. All, however, agreed that Cîteaux must find a way to extricate itself from all financial obligations toward Saint-Germain.

On his return to Cîteaux, the abbot consulted his community on the practical execution of the project. It was agreed upon that a sum of 25,000 *livres* might be sufficient to satisfy Saint-Germain, although none of the various proposals of Cîteaux concerning the investment of the amount pleased the Parisian monks. There remained only one promising alternative: the buying of an estate near Paris for Saint-Germain with secure revenues matching those collected from Gilly. But such an estate was not readily available for purchase.

The king's visit to Burgundy in August of 1479 presented another welcome opportunity to Abbot Cirey, as he was the appointed head of the reception committee. He found a way of explaining the problem to Louis XI; whereupon His Majesty instructed his secretary of finances to assist the monks in the acquisition of a suitable property near Paris.

After such assurances Dom Cirey sent word to the two Cistercians in Paris, the abbot of Preuilly and the provisor of the College, to search for an available estate that might satisfy Saint-Germain. The only remaining problem was the money needed for the transaction. Since the coffers of Cîteaux were empty, the sale of all remaining silver or gold articles, including the debris of such items recovered from Besançon, was resolved. The same two Parisian Cistercians were entrusted with the task of finding a buyer for the assorted articles of precious metals. The whole collection amounted to 420 marks and 6 ounces. The goldsmith interested in the offer was a certain Martin Mignon who, with the connivance of the two monks, deliberately undervalued the objects claiming that in most cases the purity of metals was inferior. His final offer was the sum of 4,367 *livres*, far behind Cîteaux's expectations, and even farther from the amount necessary for the purchase of land in question. It turned out only later that the secret understanding between the two monks and the goldsmith had netted a dozen silver cups to the abbot of Preuilly and over 1,300 *livres* to the provisor of the College, a sum which helped him obtain the abbey of Ourscamp.

In the distressing circumstances the abbot of Cîteaux turned to the General Chapter of 1479 for financial help. Unfortunately, Dom Cirey was unable to present the case in person on account of an illness. His absence was exploited by an implacable enemy, Pierre de Virey, abbot of Clairvaux, who saw to it that the request was rejected.

For the moment Dom Cirey had to be satisfied with a political success. He was again chosen to lead a Burgundian delegation to the royal court, together with the bishops of

Autun[61] and Chalon.[62] Not only was his mission successful, but he was appointed *conseiller d'état* with the honorarium of 300 *livres* during his current commission. Moreover, the king extended to him an invitation to join his council permanently at a much higher salary.

Dom Cirey's mind, however, was on the settlement with the monks of Saint-Germain. In fact, on March 20, 1480, he signed a contract for the purchase of an estate of the Estouteville family for 3,800 *livres* in gold, a fief in Cordon-en-Brie near Melun. Further action in the matter, however, was prevented by a new attack by Pierre de Virey against the personal integrity of Jean de Cirey.

Feud with Pierre de Virey

As his first salvo the abbot of Clairvaux published an inflammatory pamphlet entitled *Déclaration des revenus communs de l'Ordre de Cîteaux,*[63] in which he charged that Cîteaux habitually misused the collections intended for the whole Order and that the abbot of Cîteaux never accounted for the extorted contributions. Jean de Cirey refuted so successfully the baseless accusations that at the General Chapter of 1482 the pamphlet was condemned and its author forced to retract his charges and beg forgiveness for his misdeeds.[64]

But this unfortunate man could not rest. On October 11, 1482, he appealed the verdict of the General Chapter and turned to every superior court of justice known to him, including the University of Paris, the Holy See, even a future general council. In January of 1483 the abbot of Cîteaux ordered Pierre de Virey to stop his useless machinations under pain of excommunication. This, however, had no effect whatsoever on Virey's continued efforts to unseat his rival.

The position of Jean de Cirey remained unassailable and his fame and reputation continued to rise even after the death of Louis XI on August 29, 1483. The abbot of Cîteaux was appointed leader of the delegation of the Estates of Burgundy sent for the solemnities connected with the succession of Charles VIII. Dom Cirey's speech delivered on this occasion was accepted with universal acclaim; it was subsequently printed and widely distributed. He received again the offer of staying at court as a permanent member of the royal council.

The General Chapter of 1483 dealt extensively with the repeated charges of Pierre de Virey,[65] with the same results. His accusations were labelled groundless and malicious, and the abbot was threatened with further censures if he persisted in his rebellion. This was, however, exactly what he did, and on January 19, 1484, he appealed again to the Holy See, adding new charges to the old.

Meanwhile Dom Cirey rose ever higher in his brilliant public career. He was again the leader of the Burgundian delegation dispatched to the Estates General of Tours held early in 1484. It was through his learned eloquence that the prominence of Burgundy was recognized among all other provincial delegations. During the rest of the assembly the abbot of Cîteaux played such a distinguished role that through him the honor and reputation of Cîteaux and Cistercians rose to a new height. The king was the first to express his esteem: while all other donations of his father had been revoked, Cîteaux remained exempt from the payment of 24 *livres* for holding the château of Saint-Jean-de-Lône.

The General Chapter of 1484, still preoccupied with the scandalous behavior of Pierre de Virey,[66] tried to apply persuasion and mediate between the principal contestants. After the fruitless efforts of the abbots of Balerne and Longuet, Jacques II, abbot of Cluny[67] and brother of Cardinal d'Amboise, together with the Grand Doyen of Saint-Vivant, attempted to bring about a peaceful settlement, but Virey remained obdurate and continued the fight before the Parlement of Paris.

When he realized that the reputation of the abbot of Cîteaux rendered him invulnerable, he decided to forge letters purportedly written by Dom Cirey against the royal government and had them presented as evidence before the royal council. The forgery, however, was detected, to Virey's great embarrassment. This could have been the moment when the abbot of Cîteaux might have launched a counterattack with devastating results, but Cirey did not wish to give the sad affair greater publicity and was still willing to forgive and forget.

Not so his adversary. Pierre de Virey sent his faithful legal counsel, the apostolic notary named Didier Garnement, to Rome with another handful of forged documents and plenty of money. He found his way to the most influential members of the curia and saw to it that the forged letters, ostensibly by Cirey, found a wide circulation, showing him to be the true villain of the affair and Virey merely his innocent victim. The diabolic plot created confusion in Rome, but the pope, before doing anything in the matter, sought further information from Paris using the confidential services of a famous authority of canon law, Ambroise de Cambray. The lawyer detected immediately the false nature of the accusations and notified the pope about the nature of the sinister plot. The conspirator Garnement first tried to commit suicide, but changed his mind and fled in panic, while the Roman authorities were ready to move against the abbot of Clairvaux.

But Virey refused to surrender and turned for moral support to the abbeys affiliated to Clairvaux. The response was gratifying, particularly in Italy, where Chiaravalle in Milan and Settimana in Florence were willing to renounce their allegiance to Cîteaux and form with other abbeys an independent congregation under the leadership of Clairvaux. Italian secular authorities and even some cardinals looked favorably upon the movement. Pope Innocent VIII sent an alarming letter to the General Chapter of 1486, suggesting they send a high-level delegation to Italy to nip in the bud this dangerous movement. It was no secret that the abbot of

Clairvaux toyed with the idea of forming, under his general-
ship, a new order named the "Order of Saint Bernard".

The General Chapter of 1487 unmasked the plot and took
severe measures against the incorrigible abbot of Clairvaux.[68]
More humiliating was for him losing of the lawsuit against
Cîteaux at the Parlement of Paris. At the decisive session of
that high court Jean de Cirey spoke so persuasively in his
own defense that his opponent not only lost his case but was
also sentenced to offer public satisfaction to the abbot of
Cîteaux. This took place on December 8, 1487, in the apartment of the abbot of Cîteaux in the College of Saint Bernard
where, in the presence of a number of abbots, Pierre de Virey
prostrated before his superior, retracted all his charges, and
begged for forgiveness. But the grave scandal could not be
undone by such simple measures. Under the pressure of
foreign princes and prelates, on August 10, 1487, Innocent
VIII demanded a general visitation throughout the Order.

Since the most urgent business was the disarming the
Italian separatists, the General Chapter decided to send there
Dom Cirey himself, who, however, resisted for a long time,
claiming that his effectiveness had been much reduced by his
old age and various infirmities. But eventually he accepted
the challenge and left for Italy on September 7, 1488. No
sooner was he out of France than the abbot of Clairvaux initiated yet another lawsuit against Cîteaux, rehearsing the old
charges of fiscal mismanagement.

Meanwhile the abbot of Cîteaux arrived at Rome where
he was cordially received by the pope, who granted him a
public audience at a general consistory. Hearing the latest
troubles created by Pierre de Virey, the pontiff decided to
end the feuding once and for all by issuing a bull of unifica-
tion of Cîteaux and Clairvaux. In whichever abbey vacancy
was first to occur, the abbatial see and title was to be inherited by the surviving abbot. Clairvaux's place as proto-abbey
was to be taken by Preuilly. Strangely enough, the bull dis-
counted the possibility of Virey's survival. This might have

been one of the many reasons for the fact that the terms of the bull were never executed.

Privileges Granted to Jean de Cirey

Innocent VIII proved his predilection for Cirey by extraordinary favors. A bull issued on May 9, 1489, authorized him and his successors to wear episcopal insignia (Gerard de Buxières had received the same a century before only as a personal favor), and the same bull granted him and his successors the privilege of conferring on all Cistercians the orders of subdiaconate and diaconate. The four proto-abbots received the same authorization, restricted to members of their own abbeys. This latter privilege caused much consternation among the French episcopate, but it remains true that most abbots of Cîteaux exercised their right until 1674. When the French bishops decided not to promote to priesthood anyone who had been ordained deacon by the abbot of Cîteaux, for the sake of peace the privilege was no longer exercised.

Dealing with the schismatic abbeys of Milan and Tuscany remained problematic. Most of these monasteries had been dominated by the secular authorities or had been given *in commendam* to cardinals who were more anxious to strengthen their hold on these unfortunate houses than to restore them to the central government of the Order. Dom Cirey succeeded in obtaining the revocation of bulls contrary to the interest of Cîteaux, although the subsequent negotiations by the abbot of Rigny undid much of what Cirey had accomplished.

Cirey's Scholarly Contributions

On his return to Cîteaux, Jean de Cirey published the first printed collection of Cistercian privileges, produced in 1491 in Dijon by the printer Pierre Metlinger.[69] He planned to write a history of the abbey of Cîteaux and began to work on the project in 1479, although his busy life prevented its completion. But he managed to finish the story of his feud with Pierre de Virey in the form of a dialogue between the prior and subprior, which survived in an 8° volume of 462 pages on vellum.[70.] Another work inspired by him, *Declaratio liberationis monasterii Cisterciensis erga monasterium Sancti Germani*, attests to his constant preoccupation with Gilly.[71]

Gilly: The Final Settlement

As told above, Dom Cirey had already signed a contract for the purchase of Cordon with the intention of offering it to Saint-Germain, but this failed to satisfy the Parisian monks. The abbot of Cîteaux, bent on a settlement at any price, turned for help to King Charles VIII, who in a patent of April 20, 1493, addressed to the Parlement of Paris, obliged the monks of Saint-Germain to accept the Cistercian offer for Gilly. But Saint-Germain argued persistently that the revenues of Cordon were not equivalent to those of Gilly, and over this issue a new and costly investigation followed, although Cîteaux had been so much impoverished that Dom Cirey was forced to borrow 2,000 *livres* from his brother, Pariset de Cirey, a Dijon businessman.

The Articuli Parisienses

Work on this problem was interrupted by the call of Charles VIII, who for December 12, 1493, convoked a large number of ecclesiastics in order to produce a scheme for monastic reform. Jean de Cirey and the abbot of Bonport were members of the gathering. When it was over, the abbot of Cîteaux called together at once forty-four abbots to meet on February 15, 1494 at the College of Saint Bernard of Paris. The convention was intended to respond to the king's appeal and to the bull of Innocent VIII issued with the same purpose on August 10, 1487. The result of the Cistercian convention was a reform-project of sixteen articles, known later as the *Articuli Parisienses*, approved by the General Chapter of the same year[72] and also by that of 1502.

Noteworthy among the reform proposals is the eleventh article, an eloquent appeal to abbots to work for the benefit of their communities both in word and example in the spirit of selfless dedication.

Dom Cirey used his Parisian sojourn to complete his negotiations with Saint-Germain. The Chamber of Accounts formed a committee in his behalf and proved that the annual revenues of Cordon amounted indeed to 500 *livres*, as claimed by Cirey. The skeptical monks turned to the commissaries of the Parlement of Paris, who estimated the incomes of Cordon to 420 *livres* and 10 *sous*. At this point the problem was reduced to the question of how to produce the still missing 79 *livres* and 10 *sous*. The solution turned out to be the detachment of this small amount from the revenues of two priories subject to Cîteaux, La Cour-Dieu and La Grace-Notre-Dame, and transfer it to Saint-Germain. After the approval of the proposal of the General Chapter of 1497 and after further investigation of the Benedictines, the whole affair was concluded by the treaty of May 3, 1499, sanctioned by the Parlement of Paris four days later. The settlement was far more expensive than the value of Gilly had ever been. The legal fees alone from 1479 to 1498 amounted to 66,000 *livres* for Cîteaux; the total sum Gilly had swallowed up from 1300 to 1500, was estimated at 200,000 *livres*. How much more this star-crossed property was to cost Cîteaux in the future was veiled from this generation.

THE FIFTH CENTURY
(Fols. 140-229ᵛ)

THE NEW CENTURY began with the last public mission of Jean de Cirey, who was leading a Burgundian delegation to the coronation of the successor of Charles VII, Louis XII. Shortly after his return to Cîteaux a dramatic event, a gross violation of the abbey's enclosure on May 9, 1501, shocked the abbot already stricken in years. On an unexpected visit the young wife of Philippe de Hochberg, marquis de Ruthelin, claiming the privileges of her alleged royal ancestry, had the doors of the enclosure broken open and paraded up and down for hours in the inner cloister with her ladies. The frivolous incident was followed by the ritual purification of the desecrated places.

Cirey's Resignation and Succession

By the turn of the century "one of the greatest men and one of the most distinguished abbots who ever occupied the see of Cîteaux" was ready to retire. Cirey announced his intention of resigning to Louis XII, with the request that he be succeeded by his nephew, Jacques Theulley de Pontaillier, doctor of theology of the University of Paris, abbot, first of Cherlieu, then of Bellevaux, and currently of Morimond.

On November 20, 1501, Cirey resigned in the presence of his whole community assembled in the chapter hall. Led by the prior, Pierre de Dijon, the convent accepted the abbot's decision with regrets and agreed to postulate unanimously as their new abbot Jacques de Pontaillier. On the same occasion provisions were made for rendering Cirey's years in retirement carefree and comfortable. In addition to food, drink, fuel, equipage and similar necessities, he retained his apartments in Cîteaux, Gilly, and Vougeot, with all their furnishings and service personnel, and for cash expenses he requested and received 200 gold ducats annually, the equivalent of 400 *livres*.

On February 16, 1502, Pope Alexander VI approved all the above arrangements and conditions, whereupon the new abbot made a solemn promise to live up to his obligations to his uncle and benefactor. Gratitude, however, was not among the virtues of Pontaillier and by the end of 1503 Dom Cirey complained bitterly about the non-payment of his overdue pension. The quarrels between uncle and nephew came to a sudden end with the death of Jean de Cirey on December 27, 1503. The great abbot was buried under the chapter hall of Cîteaux. His blessed memory lived for centuries. In 1716 his damaged tombstone was replaced by a new one, dedicated to "the most beloved father" by his "most devoted sons".

The Administration of Jacques de Pontaillier

Abbot Jacques, in order to prove his concern for the welfare of Cîteaux, made an attempt to recover the stolen or illegally alienated objects from the sacristy of Cîteaux during the course of the previous century. Upon his request Pope Julius II issued a bull on February 5, 1504, ordering the restoration to Cîteaux of all such articles; a laudable but entirely ineffectual effort. It was in the same year that the monks became involved in a costly lawsuit. The widow of Jean de Vienne, who in 1469 had sold Cîteaux the seigniory of Montbis, attacked the validity of the contract, and the buying up her claims cost the abbey 100 *écus* in gold.

Though unsuccessful in financial matters, Abbot Jacques continued to enjoy the honorific public role of his predecessor. The victory of Louis XII over the Venetians in 1509 was celebrated throughout France. In Dijon, the abbot of Cîteaux, clad in pontifical vestments and flanked by the four proto-abbots, played a leading role in all ecclesiastical functions. The documents describing the events in great detail have been preserved in the archives of Saint-Étienne in Dijon.

The Library of Cîteaux

The new library of Cîteaux was completed in 1509, as one may read on one of the northern windows, exhibiting the abbot's monogram. It is a handsome edifice, seventy-two feet long, twenty-four feet wide. But the contents of the library were meager; the shelves were completed only in 1680. By then the number of books had grown considerably, although the quality of the collection left much to be desired. It consisted largely of the volumes formerly in the possession of deceased members of the community. Only the manuscripts lent to the library a mark of distinction.

According to the historian Palliot,[73] Jacques de Pontaillier was the first abbot of Cîteaux who was granted the rank of "born councilor" of the Parlement of Dijon, functioning as such in 1510.

Reforming Efforts of the Fifth Lateran Council

The abbot of Cîteaux represented his Order during the sessions of the Fifth Lateran Council (1512-1517), although the surviving records reveal nothing about his specific role or activity. It is known, however, that on April 28, 1512, he asked permission to leave the Council for three months in order to preside over the General Chapter of the same year. The permission was granted on the condition that the Chapter would do its utmost to promote the reform of the Order, since it was commonly known that the Cistercians had lost much of the initial fervor of their holy founders. This was particularly true concerning the female branch of the Order. The reform-decrees of the Chapter were to be given the widest publicity, by posting the documents on the doors of churches and in other public places for the edification of the faithful. Indeed, a long list of reform-statutes was formulated and duly published by the General Chapter, but Abbot Pontaillier was more interested in his role in the Parlement of Dijon, as attested by the court documents of November, 1512.

Pontaillier's Resignation and Succession

Claiming ill health, Pontaillier resigned on October 25, 1516, in favor of Blaise Larget d'Aiserey, monk of Cîteaux and previously provisor of the Parisian College. Before his actual retirement, however, Pontaillier drew up a long list of benefits he intended to enjoy during his remaining years. He was satisfied with the annual pension of 400 *livres*, but his other demands surpassed by far those specified by Cirey. Moreover, he left the list open with the remark that he reserved the right to add more to it in the future, as needs might arise. His successor found consolation in the fact that the total of these demands "did not exceed a third of Cîteaux's total income".

The monks of Cîteaux not only approved the extremely generous terms of Pontaillier's retirement, but also consented to the postulation of their new abbot, Blaise Larget, without a formal election. Meanwhile, divine Providence shattered Pontaillier's rosy expectation of a leisurely retirement: he died within a week, on November 1, 1516.

This unexpected event prompted the monks of Cîteaux to assert their right of free election, and in great haste, but with all the prescribed formalities, elected as their new abbot the same Blaise Larget. The convent of Cîteaux, in asking the king for his consent, emphasized the extreme financial distress of the abbey in order to discourage potential seekers of the abbatial title through royal favor, invoking the terms of the newly signed Concordat of Bologna.

King Francis I was agreeable, and so was Pope Leo X, thus the new abbot was able to take possession of Cîteaux before the year 1516 was over. In the following January Blaise Larget took his place of honor in the Parlement of Dijon, seated right after the bishops.

Death and New Election at Cîteaux in 1517

Under the increasing pressure of both papal and royal courts the General Chapter of 1517 was preoccupied with the ways and means of a thorough reform of the Order, but work on the project had to be suspended on account of the death of the newly elected abbot. Blaise Larget died in Paris on September 10, 1517, in his forty-third year of age.

The fatal ailment of the abbot must have been known to the monks of Cîteaux, because the election of a successor was held as early as September 16, in the presence of the proto-abbots or their representatives. The five students of Cîteaux in Paris sent their excuses and named their proxies on the day of their abbot's death. The newly elected head of Cîteaux was Guillaume du Boisset, abbot of Candeil, who was not, however, present, and for some reason was found in Lyon on September 28 by the delegates carrying the news. He gave no definite word of acceptance and, in fact, no document exists concerning the date he took possession of Cîteaux. It is known, however, that in the middle of January, 1518, he was visiting abbeys in southern France in his new capacity, including his own Candeil, where he made arrangements for the administration of the house without surrendering his abbatial title. Perhaps he continued his visitatorial activity, for he died in Brioude in Auvergne on April 25, 1521.

Guillaume le Faucolnier and Monastic Reform

The monks of Cîteaux acted again with great haste and with all the prescribed formalities; on April 29, 1521, they elected Guillaume le Faucolnier. He was a native of Rouen, entered the Order in nearby Mortemer, and in 1517 became abbot of Miroir in the diocese of Lyon. His election at Cîteaux was confirmed without difficulty both by Leo X and by Francis I.

The most urgent problem was still the reform of the Order. In the last year of Abbot Boisset, the General Chapter of 1520 dispatched Abbot Edmond de Saulieu of Clairvaux to Rome to urge the pope to facilitate the movement of religious renewal. Leo X answered by the brief of February 5, 1521. The short document listed the most obvious abuses, such as the arbitrary rule and ostentatious luxury of abbots, lack of efficacious visitation, lax observance of monastic enclosure. The pope urged the proper education of monks, particularly in Holy Scripture, love of simplicity, and generally faithful obedience to the Rule of Saint Benedict. If such reforms were not carried out soon, ecclesiastical punishments or even the "secular arm" were to be invoked.

Wise as these observations and warnings might have been, they remained ineffectual simply because the General Chapter was composed of the chief offenders. The death of the pope in the same year was only the final blow to success.

In some chronicles one may read that Francis I, his queen and numerous court officials visited Cîteaux in June of the same year, 1521. This information, however, is erroneous, for during that time the king was with his army in Flanders and the queen was pregnant and unable to undertake such a long journey.

The Alienation of Toutenant

Cîteaux suffered a serious loss of property during Faucolnier's abbacy. Philippe Chabot, admiral of France and governor of Burgundy, cast an envious eye on Toutenant, one of the earliest and still profitable granges of Cîteaux. There was no way to resist a personage of such power. Although the admiral offered another property in exchange and the annual rent of 400 *livres*, all this was a pitiful compensation for the extorted concession; the contract was signed on September 16, 1532. Toutenant consisted then of 1,300 *journaux*[74] of land, 595 *soitures*[75] of meadows in two tracts, 612 *arpens*[76] of forests, and a number of dwellings, barns, and storehouses.

In 1533 the remains of Alberic, Stephen Harding, and of some other holy founders of Cîteaux were exhumed, collected into nine boxes and placed under the altar near the door leading to the great cloister. The altar was renamed after Saint Stephen.

Between 1528 and 1534 the weather was so bad throughout France that the results of the drought were felt everywhere. Even the abbot of Cîteaux was forced to purchase wine for his monks. But as 150 *queues*[77] were shipped on barges down the Saône, the brothers were made to pay over thirteen *livres* in taxes. The abbot, claiming the ancient tax-exemption of Cîteaux, turned for justice to Dijon, where the Parlement forced the tax-collectors to return the money and to pay the expenses of the lawsuit.

But the zeal of Faucolnier for the welfare of his abbey was frustrated by the war which broke out between King Francis I and the Emperor Charles V. In fact, the death of the abbot on March 26, 1540, opened a new era of tragic reverses in the history of Cîteaux.

The Troubled Election of Jean Loysier

No sooner were Abbot Faucolnier's eyes closed than the officials of Dijon, together with their military escort, marched into Cîteaux and, invoking the terms of the Concordat of Bologna, not only demanded a year's income from the abbey, but also tried to prevent the election of a new abbot, insisting that the appointment of an abbot was a royal privilege. Nevertheless, the monks precipitated an election within four days, on March 30. The proto-abbots could not arrive, but a number of other dignitaries from nearby communities witnessed the event. The newly elected abbot was Jean Loysier, a native of Seurre sur Saône, professed member of Cîteaux, doctor of theology of Paris, who at the time of his election lived still in the Parisian College. The convent commissioned Antoine de Beaune, the purser of the abbey, to hurry to Paris and announce to Loysier the happy news. This he did on April 8, at seven in the morning, in front of official witnesses. The surprised candidate asked for three hours of prayerful reflection, after which he accepted the election. He turned immediately to Pope Paul III for the confirmation of his election, which was granted on May 16, 1540, on the condition that Francis I find him equally acceptable. The investigation of the matter at the royal court took a long time and it was only on April 30, 1542, that Loysier could take possession of the see of Cîteaux. This act, however, did not end the occupation of the abbey by the officials of Dijon. They left the house only after an energetic patent of the king, dated March 30, 1543. It was probably a personal visit of the king himself at Cîteaux during the interim that decided the case in favor of Dom Loysier, who, as a token of his gratitude, dedicated a new bell of enormous size called "Françoise" in the king's honor.

Toutenant and Vougeot

When Admiral Chabot died in 1543, there was a good chance of recovering the grange of Toutenant. His widow, Françoise de Longvy, however, demanded the extension of the exploitation of this land during her lifetime. Since she had powerful friends, among them her brother, the Cardinal de Givry who was also bishop of Langres, Dom Loysier could not resist and the grange was granted to her under the same conditions her husband had enjoyed.

The abbot of Cîteaux wished to perpetuate his memory by leaving behind monuments to his fine taste. He had a pair of ornate organ-chests and a canopy of exquisite embroidery made. Both pieces became objects of admiration to all visitors. His relations with his own monks, however, were less than cordial. In 1563 his subjects turned to King Charles IX with the complaint that their abbot carved out of the meager revenues of Cîteaux a portion for his exclusive use (*manse séparée*), a distasteful novelty in the history of the abbey. The king's answer was that the ancient statutes and customs must be observed. As if the château of Gilly were not enough for him, Loysier constructed another one at Vougeot and spent most of his remaining years there. He died in his favorite residence, alienated from his monks, on December 26, 1559.

The Election of Louis de Baissey

Reacting to the news, the monks held an election within the shortest possible time and on January 6, 1560, offered the see of Cîteaux to Louis de Baissey, who was already abbot of Maizières and member of an illustrious noble family. The official approval of the choice was surprisingly smooth and fast: Pope Pius IV issued his bull on March 7, followed shortly by the consent of King Francis II. Dom Baissey took possession of Cîteaux by proxy on September 8, 1560.

The Problem of Spanish Separatism

His first task was to counteract the movement inspired by King Philip II of Spain aiming at the separation of the Spanish Cistercian houses from their French father-abbots by forming a national congregation under an independent abbot general. Philip justified the move by pointing out that the abbots of Cîteaux were no longer freely elected by the monks, but had become the creatures of the king of France. He found the papal curia sympathetic and had already obtained a bull in approval of the project.

Baissey decided that the best way to prevent the schism was his personal intervention in Rome, although he found the coffers of Cîteaux so short of money that he had to borrow the expenses of the trip. In Rome he was received in an open consistory and quickly obtained a new bull revoking the one granted to the Spaniards. After having achieved this, he joined the Council of Trent, then in session.

Growing Financial Stress

Meanwhile the financial condition of Cîteaux was further deteriorating because of the extraordinary policies of Charles IX. His edict of May 26, 1563, under threat of the confiscation of ecclesiastical property, demanded an enormous sum from the French clergy, to which Cîteaux, too, had to contribute. The abbey's position further deteriorated by the claim of Léonor Chabot, son of the admiral, who after the death of his mother demanded that the grange of Toutenant be granted to him on the same condition his parents had held it. Since Abbot Baissey was absent and Chabot had many influential friends, Toutenant, evaluated at 19,820 *livres*, was transferred to Léonor Chabot on January 19, 1564.

This misfortune was followed by the death of Louis de Baissey on his way back from the Council of Trent, on June 15, 1564, in Pogliola, a Cistercian convent of nuns in Piedmont.

Another Turbulent Succession: Jérôme de la Souchière

As soon as the news of the death reached Dijon, Jean Peyrot, the treasurer of Burgundy, ordered the seizure of all revenues of Cîteaux, claiming them for one year in behalf of the king. In spite of this move, the monks on July 1 elected to the vacant see Jérôme de la Souchière, professed monk of Montpeyroux in Auvergne and then abbot of Clairvaux, another Cistercian participant of the Council of Trent. While he sought his recognition in the royal court, Jean Peyrot ruled the abbey with his administrators, procurators, and controllers. But the monks were not idle either: they proceeded against Léonor Chabot before the lieutenant of the bailiwick of Chalon, in order to regain control over Toutenant. The outcome of the lawsuit was that Chabot recognized the Cistercian ownership of the property, although he retained the right of its exploitation for eight more years.

Next the monks turned against the royal administrators of Cîteaux. They presented a well composed memoir addressed to the king, whom they found in Avignon. They argued convincingly that Cîteaux was not the property of its abbot, but belonged to the whole community. Therefore the vacancy of the abbatial see did not constitute a vacancy in ownership and for the same reason the monks of Cîteaux were entitled to the administration of their abbey at all times.

The king agreed, and on October 15, 1564, ordered the restoration of all revenues of the abbey to the community. For some reason, however, neither the papal bull nor the royal approval were accorded Souchière until July 19, 1566. Moreover, he took possession of Cîteaux only two years later, on May 22, 1568, and even then he did so by proxy.

The strange delays, however, had apparently nothing to do with Souchière's reputation; on March 24, 1569, he received the cardinal's hat with the privilege of retaining the abbatial titles of both Clairvaux and Cîteaux. He soon made the best use of his high position in a new confrontation with Philip II of Spain, who wished to suppress the rich abbey of Vaucelles and unite its goods with the archbishopric of Cambrai. Souchière converted the issue to a matter of international diplomacy. French pressure in Rome managed to secure the existence of Vaucelles, although the abbey was compelled to subsidize Cambrai by the annual payment of 40,000 *livres*.

Cardinal Souchière died in Rome on November 10, 1571, without ever setting up his residence in Cîteaux. He was, in fact, commonly known as "the Cardinal of Clairvaux".

Complications of the Succession of Nicolas Boucherat I

In order to avoid the danger of the appointment of a new abbot either by Rome or by Paris, the monks of Cîteaux as early as December 12, 1571, elected Nicolas Boucherat as their new abbot. He had served previously as prior of Reclus near Troyes, was doctor of theology and currently procurator general in Rome, who as such had taken part in the Council of Trent. Boucherat received the news of the election on December 25 in the Cistercian abbey of Casanova in Piedmont and after two days of deliberation gave his consent. On January 13, 1572, Pope Pius V recognized Boucherat as abbot of Cîteaux, though not by virtue of his election, but by papal provision. The pope argued that since Souchière had died in Rome, he was entitled to create the successor. The unhappy monks implored the pontiff to change the terms of the bull, but he remained inflexible. He was afraid that any uncertainty in the matter might lead to the royal appointment of a commendator.

As a further clarification of the situation, Pius V, on February 26, 1572, wrote a letter to Charles IX, reminding him that the see of Cîteaux, together with those of her first four daughters, had never been subject to royal appointment, and that all five should remain elective offices, therefore Dom Boucherat must be confirmed as abbot of Cîteaux and Dom Lupin de Myre as abbot of Clairvaux. The immediate background of this papal letter was the rumor that Charles IX had already promised the abbacy of Clairvaux to the cardinal of Rambouillet, his Roman ambassador.

The reaction of the king was that he neither confirmed Boucherat nor appointed a new abbot, but considered the see vacant and appointed a royal procurator for the administration of Cîteaux's financial affairs.

Since the monks' appeal to the Parlement of Dijon was fruitless, they attempted to approach the king directly. They complained about the behavior of the procurator and his armed escort, a bunch of ruffians who scaled the walls of the abbey with drawn swords, to the great scandal of all witnesses. They pointed out (with some exaggeration) that the abbot of Cîteaux was the head of two thousand houses of both sexes, and that if the vacancy were to last much longer, foreign abbeys might renounce their allegiance to Cîteaux. It was, therefore, in the interest of the crown to put an end to the intolerable condition and restore the legitimate government at Cîteaux.

The argument made an impact and on August 27, 1572, Charles IX revoked the commission of the procurator, a certain canon of Pagny named Claude Berget, recognized the election of Boucherat, and transferred all powers over Cîteaux to him. Only Pius V remained adamant and insisted on his right to appoint an abbot for Cîteaux as Sixtus IV had done after the death in Rome of Abbot Himbert Martin.

It is uncertain whether he ever received his bull from Rome, but from this point on Nicolas Boucherat effectively took over the government of Cîteaux, which soon found itself in the midst of the bloody civil war then raging in France.

Cîteaux in the Civil War

On January 20, 1576, Casimir, count palatine and duke of
Bavaria, about to enter with his army into Burgundy, issued
a proclamation demanding from the population support and
maintenance for his troops and the delivery to him of all
taxes ordinarily due the French government. He demanded
obedience under martial law and ordered Abbot Boucherat
immediately to pay him 10,000 *écus*.

The terrified Boucherat sought safety within the walls of
Dijon, where he managed to collect 3,000 *écus*, with which
he hoped to save at least Cîteaux, Gilly, and Vougeot from
destruction. On January 24, the amount was handed over to
a certain Captain de Lenty. In the sequel the troops did
occupy Cîteaux and its possessions, consumed the victuals
found in them, but, apparently, left the buildings intact.

As if these calamities were not enough, Léonor Chabot
renewed his claims over Toutenant under the pretext that
Cîteaux owed him no less than 22,175 *livres* of unpaid debt.
Boucherat, under heavy pressure and obligation to feed his
starving monks, bowed to the inevitable and on June 14,
1576, sold Toutenant to Chabot for 30,000 *livres*, although
on account of the abbey's outstanding debt, he netted only
7,825 *livres*. Since this did not cover the needs of Cîteaux,
Boucherat in the same year sold the abbey's properties in the
villages of Aubigny and Magny to M. Jacot, president of
the chamber of accounts. For the lamentable alienation of
the ancient patrimony of Cîteaux it would be unfair to
blame Boucherat and his monks alone; it was the sad result
of reckless spending and inept administration over many
generations.

"Born Membership" in the Parlement of Dijon

It was of small comfort that Boucherat revived the membership of the abbot of Cîteaux in the Parlement of Dijon.
After several of his immediate predecessors paid no attention
to this largely honorary office, Boucherat went to Paris and

on January 11, 1578, obtained from King Henry III a patent which insured for him and all his successors membership in the Parlement of Dijon as "born" councilors, recognized as such in Dijon on May 12, 1578. Boucherat soon scored another social success: he led a delegation of the Estates of Burgundy to the royal court, where he delivered a long and eloquent speech for the king's delight, although nothing is known about the success of the delegation, i.e., the possible reduction of taxes in Burgundy.

A New High Altar for Cîteaux

Finding the old high altar of Cîteaux plain and out of style and wishing to prove to posterity his taste for art, Boucherat erected a great retable featuring columns and figures of copper twenty-five feet tall, weighing altogether some ten tons, at the cost of 11,400 *livres*. At the foot of the same altar he prepared on the Gospel side a tomb for himself which bore his own lifesize statue, made also of copper, for an additional 900 *livres*.

Boucherat's Resignation and Succession

Toward the end of 1583, feeling his strength ebbing away, Boucherat resigned, but not before insuring himself an annual pension of 1,200 *écus*. In 1584 he bought for Cîteaux a mill in Gilly as the financial foundation of anniversary masses for himself in perpetuity. Although it was very strange that a monk vowed to poverty could make such an arrangement, the servile General Chapter of the same year accepted the mill with the attached obligation.

The abbatial election was held on June 13, 1584, and resulted in the promotion of Edmond de la Croix, native of Troyes, professed member of Clairvaux, doctor of Paris, then abbot of Châtillon near Verdun, who in 1581 had acted in Poland as visitor and reformer by papal commission. Shortly before his election in Cîteaux, he became abbot of Pontigny by papal provision.

The king who, on January 2, 1584, had already agreed to the resignation of Boucherat, accepted the election of de la Croix, with the stipulation that within two years he would pass the abbacy of Pontigny to a qualified member of his Order. On the same day Henry III wrote to Pope Gregory XIII in behalf of the new abbot of Cîteaux and instructed his Roman ambassador to expedite the matter in the curia. On his part Edmond de la Croix declared in writing his willingness to live up to the conditions of his predecessor's resignation. It is obvious from this letter that the cash payment of 1,200 *écus* was only a fraction of Boucherat's "pension", for it was augmented by other revenues, contributions, and privileges of all sorts, amounting altogether to twice the value of the original sum.

De la Croix obtained his papal bull on August 24, 1584, although it is not known when he took possession of Cîteaux. He took his oath of fidelity to the king on October 12, 1585 and was received in the Parlement of Dijon on May 20, 1586. By then Nicolas Boucherat enjoyed his retirement no longer; he died on March 12, 1586.

The Sack of Cîteaux

The abbot of Cîteaux attended the Estates General at Blois in 1588, which ended with the assassination of Henry, duke of Guise, that set the whole country aflame. Returning to Cîteaux, de la Croix found Burgundy occupied by the troops of the duke of Mayenne, whose captain in control of Dijon promptly extorted from Cîteaux 300 *écus*. Meanwhile the monks themselves had to provide for their elementary needs from borrowed money, thanks to the squandering of the abbey goods for foolish display by Nicolas Boucherat.

Under threat of dire conesquences, Cîteaux had to pay on April 10, 1589, another large sum to the same army; moreover in May of the same year the leaders of the Catholic League dispatched a garrison for the defense of Cîteaux. For over a month Cîteaux provided for the soldiers, but, upon the request of de la Croix, on July 25, 1589, the supreme command of the League promised to pay for the garrison and reimburse Cîteaux for what the abbey had previously paid.

The Huguenot forces under the leadership of the count of Tavannes, ensconced in Saint-Jean-de-Lône, merely waited for an opportunity to fall on Cîteaux. It arrived on October 17, 1589, while the unsuspecting monks were celebrating the anniversary of the dedication of their church. The subsequent destruction was systematic and total. Not only was the church looted and desecrated, but the abbey proper was also stripped of all movables, including the thirty-seven rooms of the well-furnished hospice; only the bare walls remained standing. The copper statues of the high altar, together with Boucherat's funeral monument were carried away and melted down for cannons. All revenues of the abbey were seized by the forces of Henry IV, while the mistreated monks fled, each seeking refuge at places they considered safe. All granges of Cîteaux suffered the same fate, although Gilly, the proud monument to the abbots' vanity, was demolished only in 1595 by the forces of Marshal Biron, the newly appointed governor of Burgundy under Henry IV.

Most unfortunately, even after this disaster, the politically blind abbot of Cîteaux failed to realize that the balance of military power had shifted in favor of Henry IV, and he continued to seek help from the crumbling forces of the League. Thus, in 1592, the desperate de la Croix took possession of the abbey of Signy, and sought the approval of this most unusual move from the shadowy government of the duke of Mayenne. In the same year the abbot accepted a bull from Pope Clement VIII which authorized him to collect from all Cistercian abbeys in France half of the *dime* they were obliged to pay, and use the sum for the rebuilding of Cîteaux, a project demanding at least 100,000 *écus*. Since the country was already under the control of Henry IV, the result was next to nothing. As late as 1593, the stubborn de la Croix turned to the last leaders of the League and requested from Charles of Savoy, duke of Nemours, reimbursement for the expenses of maintaining the useless garrison of Cîteaux, and approached the duke of Mayenne for the enforcement of the papal bull authorizing him to collect the *dîmes* in behalf of Cîteaux. All such efforts became totally frustrated by Henry's conversion to Catholicism in the summer of 1593, which insured for him the firm possession of the crown of France. In 1594 the Parlement of Paris instructed all abbeys in France to ignore the financial exactions ordered previously by the League.

The monks of Cîteaux came sooner to their senses than did their abbot. Don Claude Germain, the prior, and the young Nicolas Boucherat, in the absence of de la Croix, took the oath of fidelity to the new king in the name of their abbey, whereupon Henry IV in an *arrêt* of June 8, 1594, restored Cîteaux's total control over the abbey's properties and revenues.

The Sale of Cîteaux's Patrimony

It is not known when de la Croix did offer his submission to the king, but by 1595 he was certainly in full control of his abbey, and had begun the wholesale alienation of the ancient patrimony of Cîteaux in order to start the rebuilding of the ruins of his abbey. Needless to say, since all this was done without the permission of the Holy See, it must be regarded as totally illegal and against all laws of the Order, even against the oath that de la Croix had taken after his election. He sold first properties around Dijon, then in 1597 the domain of Beaune. It consisted of ninety-eight *journaux* of land, 427 *ouvrées*[78] of vineyards in six tracts, meadows, forests, and a variety of other properties. All was sold to six burghers of Beaune for the total of 8,400 *livres*.

But this was not all. Upon the importunities of the Brunet brothers of Beaune, creditors of Cîteaux, on March 20, 1597, the abbot sold for 1,800 *livres* the domain of Pommard with its hundred eighteen *ouvrées* of vineyards and ten *journaux* of land. Within a short time Cîteaux lost in Beaune alone 2,000 *ouvrées* of vineyards, while other sources of revenues were alienated in Bronchon, Izeure, Savouges, Echirey, Ouges, Morey, Quincey, and Gigny.

One may wonder which was the greater catastrophe for Cîteaux — the pillage of the abbey or the alienation of over one-third of her ancient patrimony?

The Attempted Recovery of Stolen Articles

De la Croix made a futile attempt to recover the articles stolen from his abbey by means of a royal patent issued on March 9, 1599, and reinforced by the ordonnance of Marshal Biron. The only tangible result of the search was the finding in Dijon of two cannons made of the copper stolen from the church, and some information about the major objects carried away by the looters to Saint-Jean-de-Lône. Thus we know about a magnificent tabernacle on the high altar; about the altar itself, surrounded by six tall columns and the statues of the four evangelists standing between them; on a lower level, there stood the statue of Moses. On the summit of the retable was a pelican made of the same metal. At some distance on both sides of the altar stood a pair of huge candelabra, while between the choir stalls there was a lectern featuring an eagle with expanded wings resting on several metal columns. Reference is made, in addition to Boucherat's funeral monument, to a large basin of unspecified purpose and to a pair of great bells. The total weight of the copper carried away was about ten metric tons; other stolen metals were estimated at 14,531 lbs.

Since no articles of any value had been recovered, another royal patent issued on December 1, 1599, empowered the abbot of Cîteaux to collect from all Cistercian houses in France the *centième denier*, "one percent of the total annual revenue of all abbeys and priories". But the devastated and impoverished houses throughout the country found valid excuses for not paying anything, and so this action led to no better results than the collection of *dimes* authorized by Clement VIII.

THE SIXTH CENTURY
(Fols. 230-490ᵛ)

EVEN AFTER the disappointing experiences described above, de la Croix believed that the stolen treasury of Cîteaux could be recovered. Early in 1600 he left for Paris where, on February 26, he obtained from the royal council another *arrêt* addressed to the Parlement of Dijon, and ordered the magistrates to conduct a search for the missing articles under threat of dire punishments for all who harbored the spoils. There is no indication, however, that this attempt fared better than the previous ones.

Election of a Coadjutor

On the same occasion the abbot obtained the king's permission to elect a coadjutor in Cîteaux with the right of succession. The subsequent election resulted in favor of Nicolas Boucherat, nephew of de la Croix's predecessor, a monk of Cîteaux, a doctor of theology of Paris, prior of Cîteaux and currently abbot of Vaucelles.

In 1601 de la Croix held a General Chapter. He used the occasion to make the habits of abbots distinct from that of the ordinary monks by adding a cape and a pectoral cross. On solemn occasions, such as the sessions of the Parlement of Dijon, the abbots wore thenceforth a splendid rochet.

De la Croix's Feud with His Monks
and the Proto-Abbots

Such pompous pretensions aggravated de la Croix's relation with both his monks and his fellow-abbots. Denis Largentier, abbot of Clairvaux, and Claude Masson, abbot of Morimond, protested against his assumed title of "general" of his Order, while the monks became unwilling to approve their abbot's disastrous fiscal policies. When in Paris, he was exposed to the pressure of numerous creditors; therefore on September 26, 1601, the abbot wrote a long letter to his monks, asking for the authorization of further loans of at least 6,000 *écus*, which the religious flatly refused. When the creditors threatened to seize his horses, on November 3, 1601, de la Croix wrote another moving letter to Cîteaux asking for the same, but the monks felt no sympathy for their absentee abbot. In order to avoid further unpleasantries and ease his poverty, de la Croix decided to undertake a tour of foreign visitations, where he found greater understanding and courtesy, including the recognition of his title "abbot general", which came under renewed fire from the four proto-abbots. We find him in 1604 visiting in Spain. He died in Barcelona on August 21, 1604, and was buried in the church of the great Cistercian abbey of Poblet.

The Succession of Nicolas Boucherat II

As coadjutor, Nicolas Boucherat II took the abbatial see without election. His oath of fidelity to the king took place in Fontainebleau on October 4, 1604, and was received at the Parlement of Dijon on January 13, 1605.

The General Chapter of 1605 deplored the condition of Cîteaux and condemned the indiscriminate alienation of monastic property, but failed to propose anything effective to remedy the sorry situation. In 1606 the four proto-abbots visited Cîteaux and found the abbey so utterly impoverished that they composed a circular letter begging all abbeys to show "their compassion and charity" toward their common "mother". There is no evidence to show in what measure this appeal was effective. The General Chapter of 1609 confirmed all previous resolutions against unauthorized sale of monastic property and reminded the abbots that it was their duty to make efforts to recover their lost patrimonies. In the case of Cîteaux the resolution brought no immediate relief.

The Jesuits, Belle-Branche, La Bussière and Miroir

The depressing poverty of the Order might have encouraged the Jesuits to reach out for some struggling monasteries of the Order in an effort to strengthen the position of some of their newly established institutions. Such was the Collège de La Flèche, founded in 1607, which in 1609 made an attempt to acquire the goods of the Cistercian Belle-Branche. The Jesuits assumed that their influence in Rome was such that Pope Paul V would agree to this union, meaning the total suppression of Belle-Branche. When they met a resolute Cistercian opposition, they tried to exploit the poverty of Cîteaux and sweeten the loss of one abbey by encouraging Cîteaux to absorb the goods of the nearby La Bussière. Henry IV agreed to the double proposition and so informed the General Chapter of 1609. Thus, the issue turned out to be the destruction of not one, but two Cistercian abbeys. The pope insisted only on the maintenance of the convent of La Bussière, but had no objection to the union of the "abbot's portion" with the goods of Cîteaux.

Meanwhile Cîteaux and the monks of Belle-Branche, together with the family which once founded the latter abbey, turned to the Parlement of Paris for help against the Jesuits. On February 11, 1610, the high court decided that the Jesuits might take the "abbot's portion", but the convent of Belle-Branche must be maintained. The fathers of the Society of Jesus decided that half a loaf was better than none and accepted the arrangement, at least until 1684.

As to the future of La Bussière, new difficulties arose after the succession of Louis XIII, who knew nothing about the previous arrangement and appointed a commendatory abbot for that house. When the king realized his mistake, instead of revoking his appointment, he granted the "abbot's portion" of Miroir to Cîteaux, which, however, did have a regular abbot in the person of Dom Jean de Saint-Maurice. When the case at this stage reached Rome, the pope agreed in principle to the transfer of the "abbot's portion" of Miroir to Cîteaux, but demanded the maintenance of the present number of monks in perpetuity. On January 1, 1613, Dom Saint-Maurice declared that he was willing to resign, if his future was insured by an adequate portion of abbatial revenues, which included 1,000 *livres* annually in addition to a sufficient quantity of wine, victuals, and other daily necessities. It was under such conditions that the Parlement of Dijon issued the *arrêt* of union on January 11, 1613. The General Chapter of the same year approved the above union and the contract with Dom Saint-Maurice. Legal formalities also demanded that the union between Cîteaux and Miroir be registered by the Court dealing with ecclesiastical affairs, the Grand Conseil. Bureaucratic 'red tape' prolonged this procedure for no less than five years and the registration took place only on February 1, 1618. The historian's only benefit from these acts of investigation turned out to be the information about the size of the community of Miroir, which amounted to five priests, including the prior.

It was during these interminable investigations that Abbot Boucherat found opportunity to visit the surviving Cistercian houses in Germany.

Further Losses of Property

While Boucherat traveled in Germany, the monks of Cîteaux made an attempt to recover Pommard from the Brunet brothers of Beaune. When it became obvious that the project could not be carried out without a long and costly lawsuit, the monks agreed with the owners that the latter would support the abbey financially in the recovery of other properties, as actually happened at Brochon and Gigny.

The plan to repossess the properties lost in Beaune, however, came to grief, largely because Boucherat entrusted the whole operation to Pernot Vienot, one of the beneficiaries of the previous sale of the same goods, who, under the guise of helping the monks, actually strengthened his hold over the estate in question. Moreover, in 1622, Cîteaux lost additional properties in the village of Fixin, where a large tract of land was sold for 3,380 *livres* to a certain Jean Bouillier, burgher of Dijon. All these unfortunate dealings must be considered entirely illegal, and for this reason they were never ratified by the General Chapter.

The Beginnings of the Reform of the "Strict Observance"

It was about this time that Abbot Denis Largentier of Clairvaux introduced into his house a reform which had already been practiced in eight other monasteries of his affiliation.[79] The abbot of Cîteaux gave his consent to the movement conditionally, until the next General Chapter could decide the merits of the issue. The Chapter convened on May 18, 1618, and produced a compromise solution. Since the cardinal point of the reform was perpetual abstinence from meat, it was decided that the whole Order was to embrace abstinence, but only from September 13 (feast of the Exaltation of the Holy Cross) to Easter. The Chapter praised the zeal of the reformers but, for the sake of uniformity, appealed to them to live by the above regulation in the future. Unfortunately, this statute was ignored both by the reformers and by those who had no desire to return to abstinence at all.

About the "reform" much has been written, particularly in the *Histoire des ordres monastiques et militaires* (vol. V, chapter 41), but the reader is warned that this work is full of gross errors and distortions.[80]

The reform received a powerful impetus in 1622, when, at the request of King Louis XIII, Pope Gregory XV appointed Cardinal de La Rochefoucauld apostolic visitor and reformer of monastic orders in France, including the Cistercians. The extensive powers granted the cardinal greatly disturbed the abbots of the Order, while the reformers hoped that, with the forceful help of the cardinal, they could seize the government of the whole Order. This was the beginning of a bitter decades-long feud between the two parties, with grave consequences.

On March 11, 1623, Cardinal de La Rochefoucauld called together the leading abbots of France and promulgated a reform-decree which was substantially the erection of an independent reform-congregation made up of the houses affiliated to Clairvaux under the leadership of the abbot of Clairvaux. The intimidated Boucherat accepted the revolutionary decree, but the General Chapter of the same year rebuked the abbot of Cîteaux, rescinded the cardinal's decree as divisive and schismatic, entirely beyond his authorization, and therefore without any legal validity.

Boucherat, however, in order to placate both the irate cardinal and the disappointed reformers, on July 28, 1623, appointed a vicar general for the already reformed abbeys in the person of Étienne Maugier, abbot of La Charmoye, and permitted the reformed superiors to convene for special chapters to discuss matters of their own discipline. The first such assembly was held on July 2, 1624, at Vaux-de-Cernay. Thus, the reform as a distinct congregation, although under the authority of the abbot of Cîteaux, became a reality.

The Rebuilding of Gilly

The financial conditions of Cîteaux were still depressing, but Boucherat was anxious to prove his sagacity by reconstruction in a showy manner. Beginning in 1516, he undertook the rebuilding of the totally destroyed Gilly in the new style of the time: it was no longer a religious house, not even a fortress, but a place of rest and retreat for the convenience of the abbots of Cîteaux, who already had another château for similar purposes in Vougeot.

The Visitation of Cîteaux and the Proto-Abbeys

Another arrangement of debatable wisdom was one of the last statutes of the General Chapter of 1623, which ordered the visitation of Cîteaux by the four proto-abbots and the visitation of La Ferté, Pontigny, Clairvaux, and Morimond by the abbot of Cîteaux, accompanied by two of the same proto-abbots. This last requirement was not only against the terms of the Charter of Charity, but rendered the visitation of Cîteaux's first four daughters extremely problematic; it reduced the authority of the abbot of Cîteaux and exalted the relative position of the proto-abbots who, referring to this arrangement, habitually defied their superior in spite of the fact that this fatal statute was subsequently revoked by several General Chapters.

The Election of a Coadjutor

In the same year of 1623, Boucherat decided, referring to his age and infirmities, to provide Cîteaux with a coadjutor. Without asking the king's permission, without even calling home the absent members of the convent, the thirty-seven monks then present held an election and unanimously chose as coadjutor Dom Nicolas le Goux de La Berchère, a bachelor of theology of Paris, who at the time was still continuing his studies in that city. The strange circumstances of the election of this young man greatly upset Charles Boucherat, abbot of Pontigny and nephew of Dom Nicolas Boucherat II, who happened to be present and had hoped that he himself would be chosen as coadjutor. He left the assembly in a huff without signing the *procès-verbal* of the election. Indeed, the newly elected coadjutor was never confirmed either by the king or by the pope and the validity of the election remained questionable.

Dom Nicolas Boucherat II died in Dijon on May 23, 1625, in his sixty-third year of age.

A Contested Election at Cîteaux

The election of a new abbot was complicated by the fact that the coadjutor created in 1623 had never been recognized as such by higher authorities. Moreover, there emerged an ardent competitor for the vacant see of Cîteaux in the person of Charles Boucherat, abbot of Pontigny, a young man of twenty-six.

Over the protest of Dom Le Goux, the coadjutor, Dom François Martin, the prior of Cîteaux, convoked the members of the abbey and invited the proto-abbots for a new election to be held on May 15. On that occasion, however, the young Boucherat declared that any election was necessarily illegal until the claims of La Goux had been disposed of. The partisans of Boucherat, exploiting the momentary confusion, held a hasty election, cast twenty-three votes for the abbot of Pontigny, and turned immediately to the king for the approval of the election.

Prior Martin himself took the road for Paris, where he asked for the king's permission to hold another election, although before receiving an answer, he announced July 3 as the date of the electoral convention. The legality of this move was immediately contested by both Le Goux and Boucherat.

The convention of July 3 was another exercise in futility. On the claims of Le Goux opinions differed, and when the presiding prior pressed for the new election, Dom Pierre Folin, an ardent partisan of Boucherat, protected against any new move, insisting that on the previous May 15 Boucherat had already been elected. Nevertheless, an election was held and a majority of votes cast favored Dom Pierre Nivelle, a doctor of theology and then abbot of Saint-Sulpice. On the next day, July 4, a delegation of the monks left for Paris to obtain the necessary royal approval for Nivelle. A letter addressed by them to Cardinal La Rochefoucauld disclosed more about the abbot-elect. Nivelle had entered the Order at Cîteaux some thirty years before and was noted for his exemplary conduct. He finished his university studies in Paris in 1612, served as prior in Cîteaux, then as provisor in Paris for nine years, and was finally promoted to the abbacy of Saint-Sulpice. While in Paris, he also acted as procurator general of the Order, and spent two years in Rome in a similar capacity.

The king, having received several contradictory requests, decided to entrust the matter to a committee and on August 11 appointed for the interim a caretaker for the goods of Cîteaux, Jacques Bossuet, councilor of the Parlement of Dijon, a man closely associated with Boucherat's party.

Under pressure from Boucherat, the king on August 25 issued an *arrêt* which annulled the previous elections and ordered another to be held in the presence of the bishops of Langres[81] and Chalon[82] and a high-ranking royal official. They in turn designated November 3 as the date of the third and final election. Abbot Boucherat made the best use of the time still available to him. He electioneered actively among the young students of Cîteaux in Paris by granting them all sorts of personal favors. Wishing to continue the same, he arrived at Cîteaux earlier than the designated date. When the gates were not immediately opened to him, he threatened to have them broken down, and after he got inside, he held secret meetings with his followers.

Pierre Nivelle, however, easily won again, by thirty-eight votes against twenty-six cast for Boucherat. The disappointed loser left Cîteaux immediately, without signing the *procès-verbal* and ready to appeal the legality of the election in Rome. The king saw no reason to withhold his approval of Nivelle's election and issued his patent on January 16, 1626. But Boucherat's appeal on the previous December 5 might have prolonged considerably Nivelle's acceptance in Rome. The monks of Cîteaux turned again to Louis XIII, who on April 8, 1626, instructed his Roman ambassador to expedite Nivelle's bull. This document did not survive, but it is known that the new abbot took his oath of loyalty to the king on September 25, 1626, and on December 14 he was received at the Parlement of Dijon.

The time, effort, and money spent in behalf of Nivelle were all wasted. He proved to be a violent, capricious, and vindictive superior, without compassion or charity toward his subjects.[83]

Approval of the Reform

As soon as Nivelle took full charge of Cîteaux, the leaders of the reform turned to him with a request he confirm the concessions granted them by Nicolas Boucherat II. Nivelle complied, and on February 6, 1628, confirmed Étienne Maugier as the vicar of the reform, although he emphasized that in matters of discipline, for the sake of uniformity, abstinence should be their only distinction. The General Chapter of the same year approved this arrangement and recognized the legitimate status of the reform in all houses in which it was already practiced.

Nivelle's Feuding with His Monks

In spite of his impressive credentials, Nivelle was in trouble with his community as soon as he asked approval for a loan of 6,000 *livres* to cover the expenses of his prolonged legal battle for recognition as abbot of Cîteaux. Eventually, instead of the amount agreed upon, he took 7,000 *livres*. Several monks refused to ratify the contract, whereupon Nivelle carved out the "abbot's portion" from the rest of monastic income and handled it independently without giving attention to the needs of the community.

On September 5, 1629, thirty of his unhappy subjects presented him with a long remonstrance, pointing out that conditions in the house had deteriorated to a dangerous degree and that the whole Order was facing total ruin unless he was willing to heed his monks' warnings. They objected to his scandalous fiscal administration; the lack of proper consultation with monastic officials; the mounting debts of the abbey; his useless building and remodeling projects; the maintenance of superfluous service personnel, such as a painter, embroiderer, and carpenter. They demanded charitable treatment for the monks: giving them a servant, a horse, and sufficient money when traveling. They insisted that young monks be sent for studies to Paris and at least fifty monks be kept permanently in Cîteaux. They complained about the ruinous condition of the infirmary, which was made particularly embarrassing by the fact that in the absence of accommodations for guests, even strangers were sleeping together with the sick monks. Considering that the monks rose early (between two and three on weekdays; even earlier on feasts) and that the first meal was served at eleven, they asked permission to have a glass of wine in the morning. They asked consideration for the infirmities of the monks, so that they should not depend on the help of their parents. They reminded him of his duties of visitation, of maintaining a properly organized novitiate, of performing the customary liturgical duties, of inflicting severe punishments only with the consent of his council. Finally, the monks warned him that because of total neglect, some abbeys might seek support under diocesan jurisdiction or even in secularization. The document closed with the demand for a written answer within a week.

Nivelle had no intention of complying. Instead, in cold fury, he stormed into the next morning's chapter and on the spot deposed Dom Pierre Regnault, the cellarer, whom he suspected of being the chief mover behind the conspiracy. The dissident monks, however, refused to be intimidated and turned to both the Parlement of Dijon and Pope Urban VIII for justice.

On September 15 the Parlement issued an *arrêt* restoring

Regnault to his office, prohibiting Nivelle from removing anyone from his position, and sending a lay councilor to Cîteaux to investigate the charges.

The official arrived at Cîteaux on September 21 and stayed in the house until October 19, while he listened to the damaging testimonies of twenty-seven monks and lay-brothers. The complaints were about the same as listed in the above document, with the addition of a number of concrete details. Thus, a certain Brother Michel Bichot complained that he was denied a second habit, while the only one he had turned to a fleabag. It was reported that another brother in the middle of a cold winter asked for a pair of of long pants. After they were denied him his legs were so badly frozen that he died without ever receiving proper attention. It was charged that Nivelle craved money so much that he accepted substantial amounts from novices and from parents of young monks, ostensibly for their university education, although in fact he sent no students to Paris. Meanwhile he spent money foolishly, converting windows to doors and doors to windows, breaking down or erecting partition walls, so that he was in debt for at least 26,000 *livres*. In his vanity he put his coat of arms (which he changed several times) everywhere; once he paved a whole room with tiles bearing his crest. He perfumed his garments, kept scented flowers in his apartment. His table was laden with rare delicacies which he shared with his servants. He gave horses to his lackeys, but denied the same to his monks. Once he forced an old monk to go out to Vougeot on foot. On the other hand, he was so miserly that he reduced the number of candles for funerals and masses and discontinued the old custom of serving meals to a poor man for thirty days after the death of a member of the community. He occupied himself with nothing more useful than changing and rearranging the furniture of his rooms. He rarely attended the Divine Office, and when he did, he merely created a disturbance. He discussed highly confidential matters with his servants. His neglect of convents under his jurisdiction led to the desertion from the Order of Port-Royal, Lys, and Meaux.[84]

The Reform Goes On the Offensive

Meanwhile, exploiting the scandalous administration of Nivelle, the reform decided that the time was ripe for capturing the leadership of the Order in France. Their chances of success had greatly improved. One of the reformed monks, Jean Jouaud, abbot of Prières, served as secretary to Cardinal Richelieu for religious affairs; the old Cardinal de La Rochefoucauld was eager to settle a score with Cîteaux; and Louis XIII remained as interested in monastic reform as ever. After the reformed abbots had taken the initiative, on September 10, 1632, Urban VIII granted to La Rochefoucauld another term of visitatorial authority over Cistercians.

La Rochefoucauld was ready to call together a convention of leading Cistercian abbots in the fall of 1633, but Nivelle and the proto-abbots were most reluctant to appear before him. Finally, on February 18, 1634, the irate cardinal held a consultation without Nivelle and his colleagues, but in the presence of several reformed Cistercian abbots and eminent representatives of other reformed orders. It was then that, inspired by the leaders of the Cistercian reform, the plan for the takeover of Cîteaux emerged, together with other measures amounting to the forcible reformation of the whole Order.

Nivelle reacted by convoking the General Chapter for May 15 of 1634, on the assumption that he would find, particularly among foreign abbots, powerful support against La Rochefoucauld. On March 20, however, a royal *lettre de cachet* forced the cancellation of the Chapter and ordered Nivelle and the proto-abbots to appear before the cardinal without delay. The meeting took place in Paris on May 5, when Nivelle himself produced a detailed project for a general reform, only to have it rejected by the cardinal.

On May 9, La Rochefoucauld visited the College of Saint

Bernard, accompanied by two bishops and two lay councilors of state and protected by an armed guard. The visit was certainly far from a "canonical" visitation, moreover, for to the cardinal's great disappointment, he failed to uncover the flagrant abuses that might have justified his strange behavior.

Now, however, Nivelle had a demonstrable case against La Rochefoucauld, and on August 2, turned to the Holy See for justice, reminding the Roman authorities of the statutes of the General Chapter of 1623 and the *arrêt* of the Parlement of Paris of 1625, which annulled the cardinal's previous visitatorial powers. In another appeal addressed to the king, Nivelle vowed to champion a reform himself, which, he said, he had been so far unable to execute because of the cardinal's undue and illegal interference.

The center of attention, however, soon turned out to be a widely circulated document, entitled *Projet de Sentence*, issued by La Rochefoucauld and his reformed advisors. It bore the date July 27, 1634, although the agents of the non-reformed "common observance", Dom Pierre Wiart and Dom Jean Tédenat, received it only in September of 1635, and they claimed that, for tactical reasons, it had been antedated a year.

The printed document of thirty-one articles created a great sensation, for it included the virtual deposition of the leading abbots in France and the gradual introduction of reformed monks in the same key abbeys, including Cîteaux. All other representative officials were to be replaced by reformed monks; only reformed communities were authorized to receive novices; therefore it was expected that within a generation the reformed "Strict Observance" would triumph everywhere.

It is uncertain whether in this critical situation Nivelle and his fellow-abbots sought the support of Richelieu, or Richelieu first offered his assistance against the *Projet* of La Rochefoucauld. The fact is that on March 25, 1635, a meeting took place between the leading abbots and Richelieu in the abbey of Royaumont, resulting in a new set of reform-articles. This document, although it urged a thorough reform, said nothing about the deposition of abbots, but entrusted the practical execution of certain changes to a national assembly of French Cistercians to be held at Cîteaux on October 1.

La Rochefoucauld and his followers, in order to regain the initiative, on August 20, 1635, issued a much less ambitious and more "provisional" regulation than the previous *Projet*, and on September 6, again visited the Parisian college, replaced all officials with reformed monks and ordered all students to accept the new discipline and obey their reformed superiors.

The national chapter convoked for October 1 did assemble, although it was held without the invited Benedictine advisors and in the absence of reformed Cistercian superiors. The time was spent in protestations against the *Projet de Sentence*, against the regulations of August 20, and against the violent seizure of the College of Saint Bernard. Appeals against all that La Rochefoucauld had done were resolved and excommunication was pronounced against all reformed leaders who obeyed his illegal ordinances. On the other hand, the examination of the "Articles of Royaumont" was entrusted to a committee, and Richelieu was again approached to assist in the true reform of the Order.

Richelieu, Abbot of Cîteaux

The interest of Richelieu in such matters grew more and more manifest, particularly after he became the "general" superior of both French Benedictines and Premonstratensians. The cardinal did not keep secret his desire to add to his many titles that of the "General of the Cistercian Order". In the execution of this project he met no effective opposition.

Nivelle, since his position in Cîteaux had become precarious, was ready to step down and make room for Richelieu; the proto-abbots, in opposition to the reform, hoped that by accepting Richelieu they would escape La Rochefoucauld; the monks of Cîteaux were equally complacent, for the change was to free them from the tyranny of Nivelle and the threat of the "Strict Observance".

The date of Nivelle's resignation in favor of Richelieu is not known, but by November 19, 1635, all was prepared: in the presence of the proto-abbots the monks of Cîteaux unanimously postulated Cardinal Richelieu as their new abbot. Louis XIII approved the monks' choice and the great minister took possession of Cîteaux on January 15, 1636. On the 29th of the same month he appointed as his vicar Charles Boucherat, abbot of Pontigny, and by doing so he set aside La Rochefoucauld's *Projet*.

Richelieu's administration of the Order started on an ominous note: the Holy See steadfastly refused him the bull of recognition, since the illegality of his "election" could not be concealed for long. This, however, did not prevent him from behaving as the absolute master of Cîteaux.

Nivelle, Bishop of Luçon

As Nivelle certainly expected, his resignation in favor of Richelieu did not go unrewarded. He was promised and received the bishopric of Luçon, although his papal bull was slow to arrive. Since his position and livelihood became somewhat uncertain after Richelieu had taken possession of Cîteaux, the cardinal granted him a "contract" by which he claimed the revenues of Cîteaux for himself from January 1, 1636, but recognized Nivelle's right to the revenues of Luçon from the same date. Until Nivelle could take possession of his episcopal see, Richelieu granted him 15,000 *livres* which were to cover Nivelle's expenses for most of 1636. The date of this curious document was February 14, 1637.

The Sack of Cîteaux of 1636

There are indications that Richelieu wished to introduce the reform to Cîteaux on September 1, 1636. Any such project, however, had to be postponed because of the emergency of the imperial army's incursion into Burgundy under General Gallas. While the main body of the army besieged Saint-Jean-de-Lône, a cavalry unit broke into Cîteaux on October 26, 1636, followed by others. The defenseless abbey was again exposed to looting and burning for eight days, until Gallas was forced to retreat on the approach of a French ally, the duke of Weimar.

Most of the monks fled, while the enemy converted the church into a stable, thoroughly searched the entire building for valuables and carried away practically everything movable. This was the time when much of the archive of Cîteaux was burned or destroyed. Horses and other domestic animals were driven away or killed and the mercenaries took possession of the whole supply of wheat and wine. Gilly was exposed to the same fate, so that what had been rebuilt since 1589 suffered total destruction within less than half of a century. The monks who began to return toward the end of November found only bare walls.

The Take-Over of Cîteaux by the Reform

Early in December another unpleasant surprise awaited the monks shivering within the ruins of Cîteaux. A certain ecclesiastic, Antoine Froissart, a paid agent of the reformers, appeared on the scene carrying a letter from Richelieu which, for the duration of the repair of damages, ordered the monks to vacate the buildings and find temporary refuge in other neighboring abbeys. On December 23 the monks declared that they were ready to obey the cardinal's order, but insisted that at least six monks should remain at Cîteaux to perform religious services and say the foundation masses.

Froissart, referring to his instructions, not only rejected the proposal, but Jacques le Belin, a lawyer of Dijon and Richelieu's procurator at Cîteaux, also declared that he was in no position to furnish food for those who wished to remain in the abbey. Further resistance was made pointless when the abbot of Grosbos, commissary of Charles Boucherat, declared that he was empowered to use military force against the recalcitrant monks. After the eviction of the last man, the abbey, for the first time in its history, stood entirely vacant for six months.

Meanwhile, on July 30, 1637, Richelieu concluded a contract with the reformers, who promised to furnish fifteen monks for the replacement of the ousted "ancients". The execution of the details was entrusted to Charles Boucherat who, on September 3, introduced the handful of young reformed monks to Cîteaux under the leadership of Jean Drouet, abbot of Les Pierres, who at Cîteaux enjoyed the title only of the prior.

The fifty exiled members of the abbey sought survival either with their relations or taking the place of vicars in neighboring churches. Some had nothing else to live on but the stipends of masses they said. A few volunteered to submit themselves to the new discipline at Cîteaux, but were turned away.

The life of the reformed inhabitants of Cîteaux was not easy either: they had to live on the rent of 38,000 *livres* annually insured them by a contract which was renewed for nine years as late as November, 1642. Since Charles Boucherat, Richelieu's vicar, could find no one among the reformers who was capable of administering the financial affairs of Cîteaux, he permitted the return of Louis Loppin, one of the old members of the abbey, who carried out the duties of the procurator general not only during Richelieu's lifetime but also for a few years after the cardinal's death, which occurred on December 4, 1642.

The First Election of Claude Vaussin

This was the event the outcasts of Cîteaux were waiting for. After the news of Richelieu's death they arrived at Cîteaux one by one and began preparations for an abbatial election, in spite of the fact that Louis XIII remained firmly committed to the execution of La Rochefoucauld's *Sentence*, i.e., the election of a member of the reform. In order to enforce the decree the king dispatched to the scene M. Verthamon,[85] one of his councillors of state.

But while the Parisian government issued one *arrêt* after another on behalf of the reformed occupants of Cîteaux, the returned "ancients" acted with resolution. In bold challenge to the whole legal foundation on which the famed *Sentence* rested, they elected among themselves as prior Jean Boucherat, who on January 2, 1643, held an election which, though ignored by the reformers, gave a unanimous vote to the "ancient" candidate, Claude Vaussin, professed member of Clairvaux, doctor of theology and momentarily prior of Froidmont near Beauvais.

Since this election lacked many of the prescribed legal formalities, the reformers had no difficulty in obtaining the *arrêt* of January 21, which declared the action null and void and ordered the "ancients" to leave Cîteaux immediately. By then, however, Vaussin and his party were not without powerful supporters. The Roman procurator general of the Order in open alliance with the "ancients" presented the pope with a formal protest against the *Sentence*, whereupon the pontiff appointed for the investigation a committee of three French bishops, those of Mâcon, Auxerre, and Langres, who were empowered to act either jointly or individually.

The initiative was seized by the bishop of Mâcon,[86] who ordered the parties to appear before him immediately. The reformers, who suspected that the bishop had little sympathy for their cause, requested a month's delay, but received only one week. The unhappy leaders of the Strict Observance appealed to the Holy See and requested a new committee. Meanwhile, however, more important events happened in Paris. Louis XIII died on May 14, 1643, and the regency governing during the minority of Louis XIV was no longer as firm a supporter of the reform as the late king had been.

Nevertheless, in the subsequent manœuvers the reformers

scored a victory. On June 6, 1643, they obtained the appointment of a new papal committee in charge of the dispute. Composed of Octave de Bellegarde, archbishop of Sens, Nicolas de Grillet, bishop of Uzès, and Pierre de Broc Saint-Mars, bishop of Auxerre, the committee established its headquarters at the Parisian Saint-Magloire where for a year it was exposed to the most intensive pressure from all sides, including foreign Cistercian houses. But on June 13, 1644, the new sentence was issued, intended to be a compromise: all members of Cîteaux, both reformed and non-reformed, were to participate in the election of a new abbot, who, however, could only be a member of the Strict Observance. Meanwhile, the monks of La Ferté, Pontigny, Clairvaux, and Morimond were no longer under such restrictions; therefore the "ancient" members of Cîteaux had a just grievance when they appealed the new decision. First they turned to the Parlement of Paris, but later they changed their minds and transferred the case to the royal *Conseil d'Etat.*

The Second Election of Vaussin

The *arrêt* of the royal council of April 5, 1645, came as a clear victory for the "ancients". It found their cause justified and, making arrangements for a new election, restored to the original members of Cîteaux both their active and passive votes, although it decided that regardless of the outcome of the election, both observances must find a way to co-habit the disputed abbey, since the only material reason for division was the matter of abstinence.

Accordingly, the intendant of Dijon, M. Machault, received instruction for the preparation of orderly elections in the face of Jean Drout's constant efforts to obstruct the move. The sum of 500 *livres* was spent to cover the travel expenses of all still absent members of Cîteaux, and 3,000 *livres* were given to Louis Loppin for provisions in anticipation of the needs of the large number of monks and official guests.

Drouet, the reluctant prior, finally bowed to the inevitable and convened the electors for May 10, 1645. On the appointed date thirty-seven "ancients" and sixteen reformers assembled conjointly in the presence of the royal representative, the four proto-abbots, and several leading citizens of Dijon.

Machault brushed aside the desperate last minute protests of the reformed leaders, and after all prescribed ceremonies had been completed, the balloting resulted in sixteen votes for Jean Jouaud, abbot of Prières, and thirty-seven votes for Claude Vaussin, the candidate of the Common Observance. It was only after a new outburst of protestations and threats of appeal that finally Vaussin was proclaimed abbot-elect of Cîteaux. A procession to the church and the singing of the *Te Deum* concluded the battle.

The triumphant "ancients" announced the victory to all foreign abbeys of the Order and, suspecting further litigations in the matter, encouraged them to support the new abbot general with all their might and influence.

Vaussin's First Years as Abbot General

For the time being, all seemed to favor the new abbot of Cîteaux. On May 26, a royal patent recognized the validity of the election; moreover, the king ordered his ambassador in Rome to use his influence for the speedy issuance of the papal bull to the same effect. Innocent X, however, responding to the appeal of the reformers, entrusted the examination of the circumstances of the election to a high-ranking committee of Roman prelates which, having found the charges frivolous, facilitated the issue of the bull of approval on November 29, 1645, and by it also imposed perpetual silence on the Strict Observance.

Vaussin took possession of Cîteaux on January 15, 1646, and took the oath of fidelity to the king in Paris on the subsequent February 16. As a special favor, the abbot general obtained a dispensation that enabled him to be received at the

Parlement of Dijon in spite of the fact that its first president was his own half-brother, Jean Bouchu. Vaussin's presentation at the Parlement as born-councillor took place on April 19.

As a gesture of friendship he held a meeting with the proto-abbots at Clairvaux on August 22, when with their full support he appointed his provincial vicars and a prior for Cîteaux in the person of François du Chemin, doctor of theology and member of the Parisian Val-Notre-Dame (a house later taken by the Feuillants), an excellent choice.

The abbey of Cîteaux did not immediately benefit from the change in administration. The debts of the house remained oppressing and if Vaussin's sister-in-law had not sent a bed for him, he would have found no suitable place to sleep in his apartment.

Meanwhile, the special Roman congregation appointed for Cistercian affairs continued its work and scrupulously examined all issues that separated the two observances, including the legitimate custom of serving meat on certain days to the monks. The congregation took the side of the Common Observance and the subsequent bull of Innocent X of February 1, 1647, setting aside the regulations of La Rochefoucauld and the sentence of the episcopal committee of 1644, confirmed the decision of the congregation.

It was in this same year that a much-disputed statute of the General Chapter of 1623 concerning the formalities of the visitation of La Ferté, Pontigny, Clairvaux, and Morimond was set aside by the mutual agreement of Vaussin and the proto-abbots. On July 25, 1647, the proto-abbots admitted in writing that the abbot of Cîteaux had the right to visit their abbeys alone, and that if he decided to take along one or another of their rank, it was a matter of courtesy and by no means a legal necessity.

Still in the same year Vaussin found time to visit his filiations in Provence and Gascony. In 1648 he was elected representative of the clergy in the meeting of the Burgundian estates.

The Resumption of Hostilities

In 1649 the leaders of the Strict Observance decided that the time was ripe for breaking the "perpetual silence" imposed upon them in 1647 and to renew their attack against Vaussin. The strategy was so carefully planned that the abbot general could not escape the charge of having proceeded illegally. The first move was the resignation of the procurator of the Parisian college, Pierre Gauthier, a reformed monk, whom Vaussin replaced by Pierre de Lancy, another member of the same observance. The second step was the resignation of Abbot Joseph Arnolfini of Châtillon as vicar general of the Strict Observance; in his stead Vaussin promoted the most logical choice, Abbot Jean Jouaud of Prières, who, if not by title but in fact, had been the leader of the reform ever since the death of Maugier. Finally, the same Jouaud requested permission to hold a convention of reformed superiors, which Vaussin countered with the suggestion that such a meeting be held during the General Chapter planned for 1651.

The outbreak of the storm was momentarily postponed by a royal visit to Cîteaux on April 12, 1650, when Louis XIV, accompanied by his mother, brother, Mazarin, and a number of royal personages, rode from Dijon to the abbey, where Vaussin entertained his guests in style befitting their ranks.

In May, however, the war of observances was resumed by the illegal convention of the reformers at Foucarmont, where the delegates refused to accept Jouaud and instead re-elected as their vicar the just resigned Joseph Arnolfini. The replacement of Gauthier was equally denounced and Dom Lancy was refused the papers and keys of the college. The most obviously calculated insult to Vaussin was, however, the delegation of Jouaud to him by the reformed leaders to inform him of the resolutions of the convention of Foucarmont. Vaussin answered that he was willing to grant the audience as to a private individual, but not as to a delegate of an illegal convention.

The subsequent litigation over each of these issues was carried out for another decade both at Rome and at the various royal courts in Paris. Eventually, however, the original pretexts fell into the background and once again the validity of La Rochefoucauld's *Sentence* as well as that of the episcopal committee of 1644 came into the forefront, both implying that Vaussin's election had been null and void.

For a while there was hope that the General Chapter convoked for May 8, 1651, might settle the contested issues, since, with the notable exception of Jouaud, many reformed abbots attended the chapter and six of them acted as definitors. Surprisingly, the briefs of Urban VIII of 1635 and of Innocent X of 1647 were received without notable contradiction, although both had been issued in favor of the Common Observance. But the hope for reconciliation failed to materialize. Right after the chapter litigation flared up anew over the validity of La Rochefoucauld's regulations. Vaussin, however, was by no means totally absorbed by such worries and in 1653 found time to visit his affiliated houses in Île-de-France, Anjou, Maine, Touraine, Brittany, and Normandy.

The death of Claude Largentier, abbot of Clairvaux, on September 7, 1653, provided another occasion on which the legal validity of the famed *Sentence* could be tested. The Strict Observance immediately put up a reformed candidate for the vacant see, but Vaussin was more adroit. On February 19, 1654, he obtained a royal *arrêt* insuring the monks' right to a free election, which resulted in victory for Pierre Henry, a dedicated "ancient".

The success gave the impression to Vaussin that it was safe to leave France and undertake an extensive tour of visitation in Switzerland and the Germanies. He secured the permission of the king, a passport, and a number of letters of recommendation to local rulers and magistrates. Louis XIV with his own hand wrote such a letter on Vaussin's behalf to Emperor Ferdinand III. The abbot general left Cîteaux on

April 13, 1654, with a large suite, which included his young nephew, Pierre Bouchu, then only a deacon but already abbot of Sept-Fons, François du Chemin, prior of Cîteaux, two secretaries, his personal physician, a cook, and several coachmen, valets, and lackeys.

Although François du Chemin left behind a detailed travelogue,[87] the narrative reveals nothing about the conditions of the visited abbeys. After the great Salem and Kaisheim (where Vaussin ordained several deacons and sub-deacons), the travelers called at Schöntal, Bronnbach, Würzburg, and the Bohemian Plass. In Prague the viceroy received the guests with generous hospitality. On June 28, Pierre Bouchu, who had just been ordained priest, said his first mass at the abbey of Königsaal, where the monks were disappointed at being asked to sing the mass in Latin instead of Bohemian. After having visited Hohenfurt, Vaussin was ready to enter Austria proper when unexpected obstacles emerged in his path. He stopped at Baumgartenberg, where on July 22 he convoked a national chapter for the Congregation of Upper Germany to be held on August 27 in the imperial city of Rottweil in Swabia. On July 31 Bouchu became ill, left the party and headed directly back to Sept-Fons. While at the abbey of Raitenhaslach, Vaussin received the decision of the crown-council of Vienna which positively prohibited his entry into Austria. A confidential letter from the abbot of Heilingenkreuz hinted that the decision was the result of Spanish protest and the unfriendly attitude of the abbots of Lilienfeld and Rein.

At Rottweil the city magistrates received the arriving abbots with great courtesy. By August 30 the convention was over and as a symbol of his gratitude, Vaussin donated to the city a silver vase on which the names of all participants of the chapter were engraved. After this event, Vaussin headed home, arriving at Cîteaux on September 9, 1654.

Anne of Austria and the Reform

As years went by, the dedicated efforts of Jean Jouaud, who enjoyed the full confidence and support of the queen mother, Anne of Austria, began to bear fruit. He obviously forgot his letters of 1647 in which he had praised Vaussin's administration, his efforts in maintaining an excellent novitiate at Cîteaux and sending five eminent students to the College of Saint Bernard in Paris. He resolved to prove his adversary an intruder and take the see of Cîteaux himself. His strategy concentrated on proving the validity of La Rochefoucauld's *Sentence*. He was certain that victory in this sole issue would deliver the whole Order into his power.

Succession at La Ferté

Cardinal Mazarin, on the other hand, was Vaussin's firm supporter, as the succession at La Ferté proved after the death of Abbot Yves Sauvageot on February 3, 1655. As previously at Clairvaux, the Strict Observance tried to conquer the abbey on grounds of La Rochefoucauld's *ordonnances*; moreover, the reform approached each monk with the promise of a rich pension and spacious apartment in exchange for a vote in favor of a reformed abbot. Vaussin, however, with the help of Mazarin, proposed the candidacy of his nephew, Pierre Bouchu. The young man, leaning on the prestige of his powerful relation, was successful in a hastily held election on February 15, 1655.

Jouaud's Successful Pamphlet

One of the most consequential events of 1656 was the publication of the *Défense des règlemens pour la réformation de l'Ordre de Cîteaux* by Jean Jouaud. It was the most comprehensive coverage (442 pages) of the feud between the observances, skillfully composed and appropriately documented, of great propaganda value for the abstinents. Since it was the work of one of the principal actors, it influenced, directly or indirectly, future historians for centuries.[88]

In the same year, in the absence of bishops, Vaussin presided over the assembly of Burgundian estates.

The Turning Tide

During the preoccupation of Vaussin with matters of greater importance, the abbots of Clairvaux and Morimond attempted to encroach on the visitatorial rights of Cîteaux in the Franche Comté. However, on December 17, 1658, the Parlement of Dole decided the case in favor of Vaussin and the General Chapter.

In 1659 some members of Cîteaux must have sensed that Vaussin's days as general were numbered, and tried to insure for themselves a favorable future under the new administration. It might have been Pierre Bouchu and his family who initiated the rumors, and allegedly even the prior of Cîteaux, Dom du Chemin, had a role in it. Vaussin, without investigating the factual details, unceremoniously ousted du Chemin and packed him off to his Parisian monastery. The subprior, Jean Petit, who protested courageously against the hasty action, suffered the same fate. Vaussin appointed as prior Philibert Bezancenot, and Balthasar le Doux as subprior. The affair wound up before the Grand Conseil and the Parlement of Dijon, but the general managed to extricate himself from the troubles by granting Jean Petit the priory of Bonport near Rouen, and disarming his other adversaries by similiar favors.

Jouad's Triumph

It remained obvious, however, that under the powerful influence of Anne of Austria, the lawsuit at the Parlement of Paris was turning in Vaussin's disfavor. He tried to throw into the balance the issue of foreign interest in the matter, without results. Jouaud managed to turn back the clock to 1634, and on July 3, 1660, the Parlement decreed that the

Projet of La Rochefoucauld was, after all, valid and must therefore be executed at once, numerous papal and royal decisions to the contrary notwithstanding. Jouaud followed up his victory with further demands and on December 22, 1660, the same Parlement ordered the transfer of all novices from Cîteaux, La Ferté, Pontigny, Clairvaux, and Morimond to reformed houses, while depriving the proto-abbots of all their jurisdictional authority.

To the perplexed Vaussin it was not entirely clear what chance he had in opposing the queen mother. In a moment of despair he offered to Jouaud the termination of all litigations by himself joining the Strict Observance and introducing the reform at Cîteaux. The cynical Jouaud, however, carried away by his success, replied with the question, where and when would Vaussin begin his novitiate under a reformed master? It was then that the general realized that his only chance of survival was a successful appeal to the Holy See. He mobilized his own connections at the court and although Mazarin was close to death, he found the young Louis XIV interested in this affair of no mean consequences. On June 18, 1661, the royal council issued an *arrêt* which did not dispute the validity of the Parlement's verdict, but permitted the parties to transfer the case for final decision to Rome.

Vaussin's First Roman Mission

Vaussin made immediate use of his opportunity. He obtained the king's permission for the trip together with a passport, appointed Jean Tédénat his vicar general during his absence, and departed for Rome on October 14, 1661. He was then fifty-four years old and very corpulent, which added to the hardships of the travel overland. His company consisted of his Jesuit brother, Emilian Vaussin, Laurent Jornet, procurator of Cîteaux, François Destrechy, his secretary, his physician, cook, and two lackeys. A surviving travelogue by Destrechy detailed the externals of the trip, without giving any information on any matter of Cistercian interest beyond the fact that the general was cordially received in all houses of the Order where he stopped for a short rest.

Vaussin in Rome

Finally, on November 17, after a dinner at Castelnuovo, Jean Malgoirez, monk of Bonneval in Rouerge and procurator general of the Order in Rome, met Vaussin and his escort and they entered the city together on the same evening. They changed immediately to ornate carriages sent for them by friendly cardinals, while Abbot Hilarion Rancati of Santa Croce provided for Vaussin's accommodation in Rome.

Although the poor health of Pope Alexander VII prevented an early audience, Vaussin was encouraged by a previous development. The Swiss Cistercian abbeys protested the cancellation of a planned General Chapter for 1661, and complained that La Rochefoucauld's regulations would subvert the constitution of the Order, rendering the participation of foreign abbots in the General Chapter meaningless. The document was presented at the Holy See by a diplomatic representative of the Swiss Republic, whereupon Alexander VII on July 2, 1661, issued a brief in which he rebuked the Strict Observance for ignoring the "perpetual silence" imposed upon them, declared again the nullity of La Rochefoucauld's *Projet* and strictly prohibited any action that would reduce the rights and privileges of the non-reformed houses of the Order.

On the other hand, it was only after his arrival at Rome that Vaussin heard about another brief which the Strict Observance had obtained in the greatest secrecy through their Roman agent. It was issued on November 21, 1661, and in it the pope, at the reformers' request, entrusted the investigation of the legal status of the *Projet* to a French episcopal committee made up of three bishops, of Saintes, Pamiers, and Aleth. It became obvious that the success of Vaussin's mis-

sion depended on the prompt revocation of this brief, Jouaud's clever stratagem, by which he intended to wreck the
general's plan before it could take shape.

The Papal Audience

Alexander VII received Vaussin on November 21 in his
palace on Monte Cavallo. The general presented a written
memorandum, which the pope received with every indication of his best will. Indeed, shortly after the audience the
pontiff appointed four prominent curial prelates to study
Vaussin's proposals, under the leadership of Emilio Altieri,
bishop of Carerino and secretary of the Congregation of
Bishops and Regulars, the future Pope Clement X. Since the
new committee agreed that no meaningful work could be
done before the French episcopal commission was disbanded,
upon their request on December 5, the pope revoked the
brief of the previous November 21.

During Vaussin's stay in Rome he received substantial
moral support from many cardinals, particularly from Mar-
cantonio Franciotti, protector of the Order, and the influential Barberini brothers, Francesco and Antonio; the latter
was the commendatory abbot of the Cistercian Tre Fontane
in Rome, source of 10,000 *écus* annually.

The Bull of January 16, 1662

In Paris the reformed leaders received the news about the
revocation of the brief of the previous November 21 with
dismay, and they turned to the Parlement of Paris against it,
together with their complaints against the Swiss brief of
July 2, 1661. These appeals, however, lost their significance
when the pope issued the sharply worded bull of January 16,
1662, in which, following the advice of the Altieri committee, he not only condemned the whole reforming activity of
La Rochefoucauld, but pronounced the excommunication of
all those who would in future attempt to revive the same
regulations. The same document, to prepare a general reform

of the whole Order, appealed to all leading abbots and officials of both observances to send their written proposals to the papal committee. Accordingly, Vaussin sent out a number of personal letters urging all qualified individuals to respond promptly.

Vaussin's Return to France

After this date the general saw no further purpose in prolonging his sojourn at Rome. He entrusted the conclusion of the still unfinished business to Rancati and Malgoirez, and after a final audience with Alexander VII on March 7, he departed for Cîteaux through Tuscany and Lombardy. He noticed in passing through these provinces that practically all Cistercian houses there had commendatory abbots, while the communities lived under claustral priors appointed, generally, for six years. This, however, did not prevent them from using episcopal insignia, mitre, and ring, without having been blessed as abbots.

Vaussin reached Cîteaux on April 21, but after a short rest departed for Paris to promote the royal approval of the bull of January 16. The king, however, made no immediate move beyond appointing a committee for the examination of the document, prohibiting meanwhile any litigation in the same matter.[89]

Misrule of Bouchu in La Ferté

Upon his return to Cîteaux, Vaussin had to deal with the complaint of four monks of La Ferté that their abbot, Pierre Bouchu, was guilty of gross neglect of duty. Among other grievances they alleged that the abbot entrusted the fiscal administration of the monastery to one of his valets with whom he discussed the most confidential affairs of the house, and that he totally neglected the care of the sick members of the community, while the infirmary itself was lacking elementary necessities. Bouchu received nothing more than a warning.

While the royal committee examined the papal bull, Vaussin decided to visit his affiliations in Flanders and Spain. King Philip IV not only welcomed the general's intention, but ordered all local officials to extend every courtesy to him. He was received particularly warmly in Flanders, but when he was about to cross to Spain, he received word that the royal council was ready to consider the bull of January 16, 1662. The *arrêt* of July 3, 1664, approved the papal document, expressed the king's desire to put an end to the litigation by a speedy papal decision in all debated matters.

Vaussin and Rancé in Rome

Here the author of the *Histoire des ordres monastiques* committed the grave error of reporting that Rome invited the Cistercian leaders to come in person to the city for a discussion of a general reform, whereas it was clear from all the documents that only written proposals had been solicited. No doubt, Hélyot merely wished by this remark to justify the presence in Rome of Abbots Rancé of La Trappe and Dominique Georges of Val-Richer, who were not invited at all but were dispatched to the scene by a convention of the Strict Observance. In Rome, continued the same author, the reformed abbots were greatly handicapped by a thesis attacking papal infallibility and presented in Paris by an "abstinent" student with the knowledge and approval of Jean Jouaud.[90]

Since Vaussin's second trip to Rome had not been recorded, nothing is known either about this incident or about other details of the lengthy negotiations. We know only that this time the pope's nephew, Cardinal Chigi (who visited Vaussin in Gilly when on a diplomatic mission in France), proved to be a devoted friend of Vaussin, while the "abstinent" abbots carried a number of letters of recommendation from sympathetic French bishops.

Vaussin left for Rome in September, 1664, and returned in the spring of 1665 on an unknown date, and was present at a session of the Burgundian estates on May 16.[91]

The New Apostolic Constitution

The new reform-constitution, the fruit of years of labor, must have been completed at the time of Vaussin's return to France, but its official publication was held up until April 19, 1666. It was presented to the king by the papal nuncio himself. The corresponding *arrêt* of execution was issued on July 14; the registration of the document by the Grand Conseil followed on August 6.

The General Chapter of 1667

For the due reception and execution of this most momentous constitution[92] Vaussin called a special session of the General Chapter for May 9, 1667. This time ten definitors were elected from the ranks of the Strict Observance, but this did not prevent Abbot Rancé from denouncing the constitution, which, as he charged, contained many provisions against the Rule of Saint Benedict, even against the intention of the pope, who had been very ill at the time of its composition. On the other hand, the German abbots voiced their opposition to the excessive participation of the reformers in the *definitorium*, which reduced their own chances of being members of this executive body.[93]

The apostolic constitution intended to terminate the long feud of observances, although neither party was entirely satisfied with it. Both found excuses for not living up to its demands and many of the administrative abuses of abbots, particularly in fiscal matters, continued as if nothing had happened.

As reaction to the papal document was being registered in Rome, on January 26, 1669, Clement IX sharply rebuked the abbots of the Strict Observance for their opposition, and condemned Rancé's charges as *temerarium*. But the pope was more understanding toward the criticism of the German abbots and found the issue of the number of ten reformed definitors worth considering.

The Death of Vaussin

Vaussin wished to present this brief to another session of the General Chapter on May 5, 1670, but he died in Dijon on February 1, 1670, aged sixty-three. He was, in spite of the already mentioned human weaknesses, a great man. He administered his abbey fairly and with frugality, treated his subjects humanely and welcomed guests with generosity. He reduced the debts of Cîteaux, erected a new high altar, repaved the choir with white stone, remodeled the sacristy and enriched the whole house with furniture and other necessities. The cellars were full of wine, and he left behind so much grain that his successor sold 16,000 *livres* worth to merchants of Lyon. He acquired in Paris a complete set of silver tableware, the same which one of his successors had defaced by removing the emblems of Vaussin and replacing them with his own coat of arms.

New Elections and Attempted Murder

Election for a new abbot was held on March 29, 1670, and resulted in absolute majority (forty-five votes of the total seventy-three) for Louis Loppin, procurator of Cîteaux under Richelieu. Unfortunately, on his way back from Paris where he solicited his royal approval, he fell ill and died on May 6, 1670, aged sixty-three. He was buried in the church of the Cistercian nuns of Argensoles.

June 19 was the date of another election with the participation of the same seventy-three members of Cîteaux. The first balloting remained undecisive, but on June 20, on a second try, Jean Petit, prior of Bonport, received sixty-nine votes. He was then forty-four years old. The documents of his royal and papal approval did not survive, but in February of 1671 he was already functioning as abbot of Cîteaux. He was about to visit a monastery of bad reputation involving Vaussin's last secretary, when, on February 4, the unfortunate man,[94] in order to evade the consequences of his misconduct, tried to poison the new abbot. Petit recovered but the guilty monk fled, although he was soon captured and imprisoned at Cîteaux. The magistrates of Dijon obtained his extradition to secular justice and in spite of Petit's pleading for his life, he was executed after having been found guilty before the Parlement of Dijon.

Rebellion Against Jean Petit

Whether this tragic incident had anything to do with it, we do not know, but the fact is that a widespread movement was incited by the proto-abbots aiming against the legitimate jurisdiction of the abbot general. The chief instigator, Pierre Bouchu, abbot of La Ferté, supported by his three colleagues, intended to assert their independence from the abbot general and organize their respective filiations into autonomous branches of the Cistercian Order. They initiated artificially inflated jurisdictional fights, although it was obvious that Louis XIV, as a matter of principle, supported Cîteaux's authority.

The General Chapter of 1672

Against this domestic opposition Petit sought support abroad, and therefore convened a session of the General Chapter for May 16, 1672. The first item on the agenda was the reading of the brief of Pope Clement X of April 22, 1672, which decided the German abbots' complaint in their favor: although the constitution of Alexander VII contained the reference to ten reformed definitors, the requirement had been satisfied at the Chapter of 1667, and was no longer a matter of obligation in the future.

It was the abbot of the reformed Cadouin[95] who protested against the papal decision and insisted on the perpetual validity of Alexander VII's demand for ten abstinent definitors. Since at this time there were only six reformed definitors elected and the Chapter remained unwilling to yield, all the representatives of the Strict Observance walked out, declaring that they considered all decisions made in their absence null and void. The reformed abbots' rebellion furnished the pretext to the proto-abbots and their adherents for following them in their secession, asserting that the presence of only nineteen definitors was insufficient for the legitimate function of the General Chapter. Petit, however, refused to be intimidated and the majority of the Chapter remained in session until May 24.

The abbots of the Strict Observance turned to the Grand Conseil against the brief of April 22, 1672, and in this move they were joined by the party of proto-abbots. Petit was to face the conspiracy of a strange alliance indeed. The issue at stake was not only the validity of the brief of Clement X, but also the legality of the Chapter of 1672, with all its resolutions and appointments. The Grand Conseil, however, after nearly a year of deliberation, declined any decision in the matter and suggested that the contestants turn to the Holy See, as the matter concerned the interpretation of a papal constitution.

Understandably, the Strict Observance was highly reluctant to follow the advice. Instead, upon the insistence of Abbot de Rancé, the Strict Observance decided to turn directly to Louis XIV. It was at this juncture that Jean Jouaud died;[96] therefore Rancé himself penned an eloquent plea to the king,[97] who appointed for the investigation of the involved affair a committee headed by the Archbishop of Paris.[98]

Petit's Attempted Visitation at Clairvaux

Inspired by this lull in the feuding, Petit decided that it was time for a visitation of Clairvaux, headquarters of the resistance to his administration. He simply notified Abbot Pierre Henry to be ready for his reception on the eve of Christmas, 1674. Henry promptly refused to admit him on the grounds of inopportune timing and not being accompanied by two other proto-abbots, as was demanded by the General Chapter of 1623. The undaunted Petit continued his trip to the gates of Clairvaux, although he was held up once more by a messenger telling him he should not count on admittance. Arriving about noon on December 24, he found the gates barred and only after some time did a senior member of the community show up with the same negative answer. Not only was Petit locked out of Clairvaux, but Abbot Henry refused to come out and see him and even food and drink were denied to him and his escort. Finally, before nightfall, Petit was offered refreshments at the nearby manor of Morvaux, but he declined. Instead, the frustrated abbot retreated to Bar-sur-Aube, where composed a *procès-verbal* and pronounced excommunication of all those who had had an active part in his outrageous treatment. Needless to say, Henry ignored the excommunication and turned with his grievances to the Conseil d'État.

The Royal Decision of 1675

Meanwhile, under the growing pressure of foreign Cistercian abbeys, the king came to realize that if Cîteaux were to be awarded to the Strict Observance, her dependencies outside of France would seek to form independent congregations and thus the mother abbey's international rule would come to an end. This Louis XIV obviously could not permit to happen. On March 25, 1675, he confirmed the controversial brief of Clement X in the number of reformed members of the *definitorium* and, on April 19, 1675, another *arrêt* declared the General Chapter of 1672 valid; all its statutes were to be enforced and the traditional rights and privileges of the abbot general upheld. In case of further doubts, however, the parties remained free to turn to the Holy See.

On the same day the Conseil d'État ordered the abbot of Clairvaux and his monks to turn to Petit within a week and petition absolution from the excommunication incurred by the exclusion of the general from Clairvaux. This Pierre Henry did within the specified time, whereupon on April

24, 1675, Petit granted absolution to the abbot of Clairvaux and the three monks excommunicated with him.

Pierre Henry, however, could not bear his humiliation and offered the king his resignation, which was accepted. The other three proto-abbots came to a formal accord with Petit on all outstanding matters; it was signed before two notaries of the Châtelet of Paris in September, 1675.

The resignation of Pierre Henry did not turn out to be as simple as anticipated. Instead of resigning in the presence of Petit, he resigned before his convent, fixed the date of election and even made arrangements for a presiding official — all rights traditionally reserved to the abbot of Cîteaux. On December 14, 1675, he merely notified Petit about the arrangements he had made.

On December 18, an energetic reply from Petit declared that preparations for formal resignation and election were his privilege, therefore he planned to go to Clairvaux on January 30, 1676, for Henry's resignation, and he intended to preside over the election of a new abbot on February 3.

Bouchu's Election at Clairvaux and His Resignation at La Ferté

Perhaps in order to give a better chance for the election of his nephew and prior, Benoît Henry, Abbot Pierre resigned a full ten days after the date set by Petit (on February 13), and only after he had received assurances for an annual pension of 4,000 *livres*.

The election of a new abbot was set in motion on February 15, 1676, with the participation of ninety professed monks of Clairvaux. On the first ballot Pierre Bouchu, abbot of La Ferté, received the largest number of votes (44), but not enough for election. On the following day, however, sixty-six ballots were cast for Bouchu who thereby became abbot-elect of Clairvaux. His election insured that the opposition to Petit would continue in full vigor. Petit, in anticipation of the same, found it advisable to strengthen his own position by a visitation of his own filiation in Île-de France, Anjou, Maine, Touraine, Brittany, Normandy, and Picardy. Although Bouchu received his bull of confirmation on February 8, 1677, he gave no hint when he would resign as abbot of La Ferté. Finally, by a *lettre de cachet*, the king himself ordered him to do so no later than March 6. Bouchu, however, refused to move even after a second royal letter, written on February 26 and delivered to him personally by the lieutenant of the citadel of Chalon-sur-Saône. Since he realized that something must be done sooner or later, he decided, in order to provoke Petit, to follow the example of Pierre Henry and negotiate the circumstances of his resignation with his monks of La Ferté, and on March 1, he merely notified Petit of his decision. The same letter bore the signatures of twelve professed monks of La Ferté. As expected, Petit answered that the date of resignation was not his immediate concern, but that the act must be made in his presence and the setting of the day of election was his privilege. A further exchange of letters does not seem to have changed either abbot's determination.

The exasperated Petit turned to Louis XIV who, encamped with his army at Valenciennes, on March 16, 1677, sternly admonished Bouchu to obey his superior. On March 19, Bouchu resigned indeed as abbot of La Ferté, but, defying Petit, he did so privately in his apartment in Clairvaux in the presence of two notaries. Only after repeated royal admonitions did the truculent Bouchu realize that further flouting of the king's will might be dangerous. On May 11 he finally went to La Ferté and on the 12th he resigned in the presence of Petit. There followed the election of a new abbot, Claude Petit, whose character was not unike his predecessor's.

Intensified Fighting Between Petit and the Proto-Abbots

The issues of the decisive battle between the general and his implacable opponents were the same as before: the "illegal" claims of the abbot of Cîteaux to the title "general superior" and the jurisdictional implications derived from this claim. As the proto-abbots saw it, the original constitution of the Order was not "monarchical", but "aristocratic", i.e., the abbot of Cîteaux was to share the governing powers in equal measure with the four abbots of his first daughters. In practical terms, the proto-abbots demanded full autonomy in the administration of their respective affiliations.[99]

The erroneous nature of this concept can easily be refuted from the most ancient documents up to the Constitution of Alexander VII of 1666.

The popes since 1438 had honored the abbots of Cîteaux with the title of "general superior", specifically in the bull of Innocent VIII of April 22, 1489, which insisted that all members of the Order must recognize the abbot of Cîteaux as their "general superior" under pain of excommunication. The same was most recently expressed in the Constitution of 1666 as well as in large numbers of statutes of the General Chapter from the end of the fourteenth century to 1667. Royal documents followed the same trend and attributed to the abbots of Cîteaux the same title and authority, including the various *arrêts* issued between 1671-1677. Foreign abbeys and congregations followed suit and habitually expressed their allegiance to Cîteaux in similar terms.

The charges of the proto-abbots included innumerable incidents of alleged misconduct, some of them bordering on the absurd. Such was certainly their accusation that Petit, while hiding the authentic manuscripts of the Charter of Charity and the collection of the statutes of the General Chapter, circulated their texts in a forged version. In fact, the authorities forced Petit to produce the original versions of all these documents and searched even the archives of a number of monasteries, including the Feuillants, in order to uncover falsifications.

On May 12, 1679, the agents of the proto-abbots presented the whole documentation of their case to the same committee, headed by the archbishop of Paris, which had dealt with the validity of the Chapter of 1672. On the basis of the committee's report the Conseil d'État issued the detailed and final *arrêt* on September 9, 1681. It turned out to be a conservative document, confirming the traditional rights and privileges of the abbot of Cîteaux, but also listing the circumstances when the abbot general could act only in concert with the General Chapter or after consultation with the proto-abbots.

The Appointment of a New Roman Procurator

Pierre Bouchu, together with the abbots of Pontigny and Morimond, soon found another opportunity to provoke a new clash with Petit. Dom Malgoirez, the Roman procurator, died on October 31, 1681, and the urgency of filling this position called for consultation with the proto-abbots. Petit invited all four of them for a meeting on December 20 at Petit Cîteaux in Dijon, although, for some reason, the abbot of La Ferté chose to remain absent. Petit proposed for the vacant position three names: Dom de la Forêt de Somont, abbot of Tamié; Dom Meschet, abbot of La Charité; and Dom Mellian, abbot of La Chaloché.

The abbot of Pontigny, supported by the other two, rejected all of them on the pretext that as abbots they were obliged to reside in their abbeys and not in Rome. Since Petit was unable to persuade them that such obstacles could easily be removed, he finally named a fourth individual: Dom Blaise Leaulté, doctor of Paris, prior of Thoronet, and vicar general in Provence and Languedoc. He too was rejected and the three opponents mentioned two others whom Petit could not approve. At this point the proto-abbots left the room after refusing to sign the *procès-verbal*. Since the role of the abbots was merely consultative, early in January 1682, Petit appointed to the Roman position his first choice, Abbot Somont of Tamié.

The three proto-abbots turned immediately to the king

with the charge that their rights had been grossly violated, and that therefore the appointment had no legal validity.

Petit paid little attention to this baseless accusation and undertook an extensive tour of visitation in the southern provinces of France. The proto-abbots, exploiting Petit's absence, approached the Roman Congregation of Bishops and Regulars with their charges. This was more than Louis XIV could suffer. He instructed Colbert de Croissy[100] to let the abbots know that he would never permit a Roman appeal as long as the matter was under consideration before him.

At this point Petit found it advisable to convoke a new session of the General Chapter for 1683, chiefly in order to settle the problem of visitations of the first four daughters of Cîteaux. The *definitorium* decided the long-contested issue in favor of Petit, who was assured that he, alone, could visit any of the four houses. Bouchu, however, in the name of his colleagues, appealed the decision on the pretext that the Chapter was illegal in that it had come to session without their consent. In spite of this, the same Chapter approved the abbot of Tamié as Roman procurator.

The Loss of Belle-Branche

It will be remembered that since 1607 the "abbot's portion" of the revenues of Belle-Branche in the diocese of Mans belonged to the Jesuit College of La Flèche. Since then, because of the weaknesses of a succession of superiors, the monks have not enjoyed the best reputation. When more recently an energetic prior attempted to restore an orderly monastic life, his unwilling subjects decided to leave the Order by selling the "monks' portion" of their house to the Jesuits, who had retained a keen interest for such a possibility.

Eleven rebellious monks under the cloak of secrecy initiated negotiations with the Jesuits aimed at the exchange of the remaining goods of the monastery for a comfortable pension for themselves. They commissioned one of their own members, Dom Jean Duhardaz, to make direct contact with the superiors of the College at Angers. This took place in a local tavern.

The fruit of these negotiations was a preliminary agreement signed on February 11, 1684 before a local notary, which insured the monks of all they were hoping for. The contract was ratified by Jacques Pallu, s.j., provincial, on March 24. This most unusual act was based on the bull of Pope Paul V of 1609, which, in principle, permitted the transfer of Belle-Branche to the Jesuit College.

Jean Petit was alerted to this secret treaty by his procurator general and turned for help immediately to the Grand Conseil, which, on August 18, 1684, accepted the case for investigation. It soon became evident that the bull of Paul V could not provide solid ground for the recent Jesuit claims, for it was invalidated by an *arrêt* of the Parlement of Paris on February 11, 1610, which insured the quiet possession of the abbey for the monks.

On August 23, however, the case was transferred to the Conseil Privé, where the Jesuits wielded much greater influence than the Cistercians. After protracted negotiations the case was terminated on October 26, 1686 by an *arrêt* of the Conseil d'État. The document bypassed the validity of the Parlement's act of 1610, ignored the "treaty" of February 11, 1684, and decided the case solely on the basis of the sovereign will of Louis XIV. Accordingly, La Flèche became the owner of the whole abbey of Belle-Branche, with all its debts, income, and obligations. The Jesuits assumed the obligation for the support of Cistercian monks, for the maintenance of the buildings, and customary religious services, for the payment of 300 *livres* in perpetuity to the Parisian College of Saint Bernard and for contributing to the administrative expenses of the Cistercian Order.

The Roman Arbitration of Cardinal d'Estrées

While the fate of Belle-Branche was pending in Paris, the proto-abbots dispatched Dom Marc-Antoine de Beaurepaire, monk of Clairvaux, as their special representative to Rome, in order to promote their cause against Petit. When Cardinal d'Estrées,[101] who happened to be in Rome at the time, heard about the litigation, he offered both parties his services as mediator, and was accepted by Abbot Somont as well as by Beaurepaire. The cardinal reduced the complicated issues to two basic problems: the composition and function of the General Chapter as an institution; and, specifically, the critical analysis of the Chapters of 1672 and 1683.

After the most careful study of all available documents, the cardinal came to the conclusion that the claims of the proto-abbots were highly inflated, while the position of the abbot general was in harmony with legitimate traditions. For greater impact, the cardinal's sentence was incorporated into the bull of Innocent XI of May 10, 1686. Accordingly, the abbot of Cîteaux was free to convoke the General Chapter without the consent of the proto-abbots; voting was to be done individually and not by filiations; absent members of the *definitorium*, except the proto-abbots themselves, could be replaced by any capable member of the Chapter; and finally, in spite of any possible shortcomings, the pope declared the Chapters of 1672 and 1683 valid and their statutes binding.

Another Attempted Visit of Clairvaux

In 1688 Petit came under the impression that his right to visit his first daughters alone had been well established; therefore he announced his impending call on Clairvaux. Bouchu, however, was not in the mood for co-operation. He sent one of his monks, Charles Mynault, to Cîteaux to tell Petit in unmistakable terms that, unless he was accompanied by some of the proto-abbots, he would not be admitted. Mynault carried a written protest by Bouchu dated June 8, 1688. In it he still insisted on the validity of the statute of 1623 and the illegality of all subsequent efforts to change it. Petit paid no attention to Bouchu's arrogance and was on his way to

Clairvaux when he was halted by a sergeant who handed him still another negative message from Bouchu. The general, remembering the incident of 1674, did not wish to stage another humiliating confrontation, although in order to bring the issue to an end, he planned another session of the General Chapter in 1689. This, however, was made impossible by the war which broke out at that very time.[102] Instead, he visited in 1690 all his filiations in the province of Berry.

Petit's Last Year and Death

Conscious of the value of Cîteaux's forests and their potential exploitation, in June 1691, Petit signed a contract with the French naval authorities for cutting timber in Cistercian forests. When the general turned to his community for approval of the contract, some monks questioned the legality of the arrangement and complained about the modest financial compensation. Petit became very upset over the unexpected opposition and exiled the two loudest protesters. The latter did not give up the fight, but appealed the case to the Grand Conseil.

While Petit made preparations for a trip to Paris to deal with the same matter, he suffered a paralytic stroke. For a while it seemed that some home remedies might put him back on his feet, but on January 14, 1692, he suffered a fatal relapse. He received the last sacraments, went into violent convulsions and expired on the early morning of January 15, 1692, aged sixty-three.

Petit's was a most turbulent administration, but he faced the innumerable challenges to his authority with courage and dignity. One might bring up only two valid charges against him: the disadvantageous deal over the forests of Cîteaux; and his unwillingness to increase the population of Cîteaux. Still, he was an efficient leader of his community, kept a firm control over his officials and used the resources of his abbey for much needed construction, such as a new and spacious dormitory and abbatial residence. He kept the house always fully supplied with all necessities.

Petit was a man of regular habits, a model monk, always active, vigilant and particularly compassionate and generous toward the sick, whom he visited daily. Some objected to his affectations in speech and manners; as one of his lawyers once remarked: "He uttered even common platitudes with emphasis".

The Election of Nicolas Larcher

The death of Abbot Petit revived the solicitude of the Dijon magistrates for the safety of Cîteaux. They immediately sealed Petit Cîteaux and on January 17 they descended upon Cîteaux and began the same activity in the face of the loud protest of the monks. Finally, the king had to intervene. In a *lettre de cachet* he ordered the immediate removal of the seals and the recall of all officials as soon as the election was over. In order to insure obedience, Louis XIV dispatched to the scene his secretary of state, the Marquis de Châteauneuf. But the only discordant note came from Dom François Curel, abbot of Bouillas, who began to organize his party in the belief that he might win the election. The intendant of Dijon promptly let him know that he was unacceptable to His Majesty.

The election was held on March 27, 1692, in the presence of a number of witnesses, prominent members of Dijon's ecclesiastical and secular society. Of the fifty-eight professed members of Cîteaux few wasted their votes; forty-one of them gave their first ballot to Dom Nicolas Larcher of Beaune, monk of Cîteaux, doctor of Paris, who was already over sixty years of age. In fact, he became so exhausted and excited during the election that he fell seriously ill, and it took several weeks until he could go to Paris for royal approval, which he received on April 19. The Roman bull was issued on May 27, and he took possession of Cîteaux on July 6.

His abbatial benediction posed a problem, however. Larcher suspected that the bishop of Chalon[103] might insist on an oath of obedience to him, from which the abbots of Cîteaux were exempt. The abbot-elect, therefore, went to Paris in the hope of finding there a bishop willing to bless him, but all refused to co-operate. Finally, he presented himself to Cardinal Fürstemberg, bishop of Strassbourg and abbot of Saint-Germain-des-Prés, who had actually resided in that abbey. The cardinal graciously consented to perform the ceremony, which took place in the church of Saint-Germain in the presence of a number of important personages amid the greatest possible display of pomp and splendor. On August 23, the new abbot made his oath to the king at Versailles and on November 18 of the same year of 1692, he was received as "born" member of the Parlement of Dijon.

The Nuns of Biaches

The obviously tense relationship between the abbot of Cîteaux and the French hierarchy broke into the open again in 1693, when Larcher granted permission to a nun of the Cistercian abbey of Biaches to leave the enclosure for some unspecified reason. When the bishop of Noyon,[104] in whose diocese the abbey was situated, heard about the incident, he felt greatly offended, for he was convinced that the granting of such permissions was his exclusive right. On February 11 he issued an ordonnance which prohibited on pain of excommunication any nun to leave the enclosure without his previous permission. For greater impact and publicity he had the ordonnance printed and widely distributed.

The nuns, however, claiming that the bishop's prohibition had been abusive, turned for justice to the Grand Conseil, a high court in Paris dealing, among other matters, with conflicting ecclesiastical jurisdiction. The bishop was duly notified about the appeal on March 22, whereupon he turned to the Conseil Privé and demanded that the issue be transferred for final judgment to the Parlement of Paris. The nuns were summoned to appear before the Conseil Privé on September 22.

No sooner was Larcher informed about the lawsuit than he, too, turned to the Conseil Privé, and requested they accept him as an intervening third party in support of the nuns and in defense of his own rights in the matter under dispute. A subsequent royal decision, issued on January 20, 1694, recognized the right of the abbot of Cîteaux to intervene and ordered all three parties to present the documentation of their respective points of view before a royal committee of four councilors (Courtin, Bignon, Le Pelletier, Harlay).

Accordingly, the Conseil Privé, advised by the special committee, issued a decree on September 1, 1694, ordering the parties to submit the case for final decision to the Grand Conseil, and prohibited any litigation in the matter before other courts.

During the first months of 1695 the Grand Conseil held no less than twelve sessions dealing with the conflicting claims. On one occasion, the bishop of Noyon encountered Abbot Larcher in the hall and told him with indignation how unseemly it was that he, a lowborn abbot, dared to challenge the authority of a bishop, higher both in rank and in noble birth. Larcher, without trying to create a scene, merely answered in a modest voice: "It is true, Monseigneur, I am only a monk; but I have more mitred heads under my authority than you have heads covered by doctors' caps under yours". The prelate found it wise to drop any further dispute.

On March 11, 1695, the Grand Conseil decided the litigation. It reaffirmed the right of the abbot of Cîteaux to grant permission to leave the enclosure to nuns under his jurisdiction, although at each instance the bishop was to be properly notified.

The Nuns of Sainte-Croix

A similar incident emerged in 1697. In that year the bishop of Apt, Joseph Ignace de Foresta de Cologne, held a diocesan synod which decided that no one might enter and no nun leave the enclosure of a convent of the diocese without the bishop's written permission on pain of excommunication. The rule was to be applied even to convents of exempt religious orders.[105]

The Cistercian nunnery of Sainte-Croix in Apt, which was under the jurisdiction of the abbot of Cîteaux, found the new rule offensive and turned with the case to the Parlement of Aix-en-Provence. Larcher, who happened to be in Paris at that time, sent instructions to the syndic of the Order in Provence, asking him to assist the nuns in the litigation.

On April 9, 1699, the Parlement of Aix decided the case entirely in favor of the nuns and the abbot general, and obliged the bishop to cover all legal fees due the court.

The indignant bishop declared the Parlement's decision null and void and insisted that he was able to prove it before higher authorities. As proofs he produced two documents issued by the same Parlement of Aix in 1627 and 1628, which had entrusted the matter of enclosure of nuns to an episcopal committee. Although Jean-Baptiste Garnier, prior of the abbey of Thoronet and syndic in Provence, was able to refute the bishop's argument, the case was appealed to the Conseil d'État which, on September 5, 1701, confirmed the right of the abbot of Cîteaux and ordered the bishop to pay all legal expenses, amounting to 450 *livres*.

The gratified Abbot Larcher, however, did not wish to push his luck too far and antagonize forever the bishop of Apt, and he generously assumed the payment of legal fees.

The Affair of the Fauteuil

While involved in the defense of his rights over Cistercian nuns, Larcher repeated a question that had already been voiced under Jean Petit: during the sessions of the Estates of Burgundy should the abbot of Cîteaux be seated on the same kind of armchair as the bishops had occupied? In fact, the king, for the sake of peace, ordered a preliminary inquiry about the matter in 1686. The intendant of Dijon, Harlay de Bonneuil, conducted such an investigation in February of 1687, but not much was accomplished until Larcher revived the issue in 1694.[106]

Although both the intendant and the governor favored the request, the decision became complicated by the protest of the bishops and the claims of other abbots of the province for the same fauteuil. Moreover, as a diversion, the bishop of Chalon imposed higher ecclesiastical taxes on Cîteaux than customary, which touched off still another litigation before the superior ecclesiastical court of Lyon.

The bishops were particularly disturbed when Larcher minimized the difference between himself and the bishops, pointing out his exempt status and numerous quasi-episcopal privileges. By this argument he exposed himself to the charge that he denied the fundamental difference between bishop and abbot, committing thereby a grave dogmatic error. On such grounds the bishops turned for justice to the king, who in July of 1697 appointed the Marquis de Châteauneuf to mediate. The minister convinced Larcher to issue a clarification, in which he retracted the incriminating statements. By 1699 the litigation was still not over, when the General Chapter planned for the same year brought new headaches to Larcher, for his own monks were ready to accuse him of negligent administration to the Parlement of Dijon.

But Larcher dedicated himself with singular determination to winning his armchair by mobilizing in his favor the most influential ladies of the royal court through "Madame Palatine", the abbess of Maubuisson.[107] Success was almost immediate. The *arrêt* of the Conseil d'État of April 10, 1699, granted that "the abbot, chief and general of the Order of Cîteaux, and his successors are entitled at the sessions of the Estates of Burgundy to a *fauteuil* of the size, height, width, decoration, and identical in every way to those of the bishops, placed immediately after them in the same row".

The General Chapter of 1699

The monks of Cîteaux, however, remained unimpressed by their abbot's success at the Estates of Burgundy, and pursued their charges against him at the Parlement of Dijon. They complained about the small number of novices, about his absolutistic regime, ignoring his council, about his nonobservance of the Constitution of Alexander VII in matters of fiscal administration. Larcher managed to transfer the matter to the Conseil d'État, which in its *arrêt* of April 27, 1699, simply suggested that the grievances be dealt with before the General Chapter about to be convened.

Indeed, the Chapter of 1699 passed a number of salutary statutes demanding compliance with the Constitution of Benedict XII and that of Alexander VII, and urged the visitation of Cîteaux by the proto-abbots as well as the visitation by Larcher of his first four daughters. But, as on previous occasions, such demands were not taken seriously and remained as ineffectual as ever. Lesser issues, such as the prohibition of playing cards or dice, monks calling one another *monsieur* and nuns *madame*, and turning with religious matters to secular justice, as quickly went into oblivion as they were passed.

Visitation in Clairvaux and Pontigny

As encouraged by the Chapter, Larcher in November of 1699 visited both Clairvaux and Pontigny, and although he was admitted to both abbeys, his visitation ended with the written protests of both abbots, who still insisted that the move had been illegal, as the general should have been accompanied by another of the proto-abbots, as demanded by the Chapter of 1623. That this famed statute had been revoked a number of times by all authorities made no impression on the stubborn proto-abbots.

THE SEVENTH CENTURY
(Fols. 490ᵛ-582ᵛ)

Process Against the Abbot of Morimond

THE NEW CENTURY began on a discordant note, the sequel of a long and complicated lawsuit that began in 1697, when three monks of Morimond, actually all priors in various affiliations of Morimond, turned against their abbot.[108] Charging him with serious neglect of his duties, they wrote first to Père de La Chaise, the Jesuit confessor of Louis XIV, then to Larcher. The latter happened to be in Paris where he accidentally met the abbot of Morimond, with whom he held long conversations. The surprising result was that, instead of investigating the matter himself, Larcher sent as his delegate to Morimond Claude Petit, the abbot of La Ferté, and granted him every authority necessary to bring the case to a conclusion. Petit spent most of August of 1697 in Morimond and ultimately decided that the charges had been groundless and inflicted severe and humiliating punishments on the accusers. The luckless monks turned for justice again to Larcher, who early in 1698 promised to review the case.

The abbot of Morimond in his disappointment appealed simultaneously to the General Chapter and the Grand Conseil, whereupon the three monks turned to the same Grand Conseil with similar purpose. Larcher was not displeased with this turn of events, hoping he might shift the responsibility for the touchy affair to a secular course. But the Grand Conseil showed little interest in the matter and told the parties to settle their differences at the General Chapter of 1699.

In order to avoid further exposure of his debatable administration, the abbot of Morimond negotiated an accommodation with his accusers, promising them total exoneration and suspension of the punishments inflicted on them by the abbot of La Ferté. Indeed, the tenth session of the Chap-

ter witnessed an edifying scene of mutual forgiveness and
reconciliation.

This solution, on the other hand, provoked Larcher, since
it had entirely bypassed his jurisdiction. He, therefore, demanded that the Conseil d'État invalidate the role of the
Grand Conseil in such matters and reaffirm his authority in
this and similar other affairs in the future. He received full
satisfaction on March 8, 1700, when an *arrêt* of the Conseil
did exactly what he requested.

In the following May the Estates of Burgundy held a session, in which Larcher had his first opportunity to sit on his
new and properly decorated *fauteuil*.

Feud Over the Degree of Dom Bouhier

In 1702 the relationship between Larcher and Claude Petit,
abbot of La Ferté, was poisoned by a dissension over the
question of who was to grant permission to monks to work
for higher academic degrees? Early in that year a professed
monk of La Ferté, Jean Bouhier de Lantenay, a student at
the College of Saint Bernard in Paris, applied for permission
to continue his theological studies toward the doctor's degree. Endorsed by the provisor of the College, the request
was granted by both Petit and Larcher.[109]

When Bouhier was ready to depart for Paris, Petit changed
his mind and held him back on the pretext that the council
of the abbey was to decide such matters. The time was late
and Bouhier suspected a negative answer; therefore he turned
again to the general for support, who, on August 17, renewed
his permission. Without further hesitation Bouhier left La
Ferté, arrived at Paris on August 30, and promptly presented
himself at the Sorbonne.

The indignant Petit not only protested against Bouhier's
admission but also turned with his complaint against Larcher's role to the Grand Conseil. The issue was ultimately
decided by the University authorities on the grounds of the
immemorial practice of accepting Cistercian candidates hold-

ing the general's permission. Indeed, according to the Constitution of Benedict XII, approval for working toward advanced degrees was to be granted by the abbot of Cîteaux.

Faithless Monastic Officials

Under Larcher's administration there were several officials whose misdeeds were commonly known, yet for some reason the abbot chose not to take notice of them. On the contrary, in 1704, he rewarded the procurator, Dom Louis Fratrais, with the titular priory of La Grace Notre-Dame in Brie. Characteristically, on his way to take possession of his new benefice, he stopped overnight in a roadside inn where, as he claimed, he was robbed of his watch, wallet, and even his horse. It was most likely a story fabricated to cover the disappearance of a good deal of money, but his abbot seemed to believe it. Early in the following year the monks of Cîteaux presented their abbot with a detailed list of the procurator's wrongdoings, but Larcher paid no attention to the matter.

In March of 1705, scandalous charges were voiced against Dom Jean Étienne Sirot, curate of the chapel of the lower court of Cîteaux. As the source of the accusations was the bishop of Chalon, Larcher was more than willing to defend his subject, although the matter was serious. It was alleged that Sirot had buried in the abbey's cemetery an infant whose entrails had been devoured by dogs, and that he left a poor man dying in the gatehouse without administering the last sacraments to him. The bishop ordered the monk to appear before him, but Larcher found the demand abusive and turned to the Grand Conseil against the bishop. It was only on January 25, 1706 that the court rejected the bishop's interference in the matter.

While Dom Fratrais spent the summer of 1705 in Paris, one of the monks who knew about his questionable dealings, penetrated his office in Petit Cîteaux. There he found contracts, rental certificates, promissory notes, and all sorts of other valuables marked with his own seal, to a total value in excess of 20,000 *livres*. The monk sent word about his findings to Larcher in Paris, who promptly returned and examined the papers. Even then, however, he remained reluctant to take any appropriate measures and it was only in February of 1706 that he fired the cellarer and appointed in his place a young man, Nicolas Loppin, another unfortunate choice.

Fratrais, who was unable to account for his financial manipulations, left his for his successor scarcely more than five *livres* in cash, a good deal more in debts, empty storage and a monastery in need of everything. When he finally departed on April 29, 1706, he not only left unpunished, but was appointed provisor of the College of Dole, a position incompatible with his priorship of Grace Notre-Dame.

The Jesuits and the Convent of Belmont

When the abbess of Belmont died on September 24, 1707, the bishop of the diocese of Langres, urged on by the Jesuits of the city, proposed the suppression of the abbey and the transfer of its goods to the Jesuit College of the same town. When the Society spread the word that the house was vacant, Louis XIV, convinced by his Jesuit confessor, Father de La Chaise, issued the document needed to carry out the proposal.

Since this would have been the second Cistercian establishment lost to the Society of Jesus within twenty years, Larcher was thoroughly alarmed and braced himself for an unusually energetic resistance. First of all, in order to be informed about the true condition of the convent in Langres, he dispatched to the scene Dom Edmond Perrot, spiritual director of the nuns of Battant in Besançon. He found the buildings far from abandoned and in a fair condition. He had some minor repairs executed in his presence and, to strengthen the community of nuns, he transferred three sisters from Battant to Belmont and appointed one of these prioress until an abbess could be created. He sent a *procès-verbal* to Larcher of all his findings and doings. The abbot composed a detailed account of the true situation of Belmont and headed for Paris.

Meanwhile, to force the departure of the nuns, the Jesuits had the buildings of Belmont sealed and all sources of income seized. The sisters suffered great privations, but held out in the hope that help would soon come. Indeed, Abbot Larcher prevailed upon the Grand Conseil, which prohibited to the local magistrates any mistreatment of the nuns and assured them at least a portion of their legal revenues until the case could be thoroughly investigated.

The king was surprised and indignant when he was informed about the true condition of Belmont, withdrew his previous approval of the Jesuits' project and on November 4, 1708 issued a new *arrêt* to this effect.

The leaders of the Society, unaccustomed to defeat, decided to obtain through Rome what they failed to achieve in Paris, and requested the suppression of Belmont and its union with their college from Pope Clement XI. As soon as Larcher was informed about this new move, he turned to both the pope and the king. The latter acted immediately. On February 21, 1709, Louis XIV ordered his Roman ambassador, the Cardinal Trémoille, to inform the curia that he, the king, under no circumstances would tolerate the execution of the Jesuits' project.

Upon the further request of Larcher, on May 17, 1709, the Grand Conseil ordered the magistrates of Langres to remove all seals from Belmont and to restore to the nuns the control of all their properties. But the tenacious Society decided that they could wait for a further opportunity and, wishing to leave a door open for action in the future, did their best to prevent the election of a new abbess. However, even their last hope was shattered when, upon the request of Larcher, on November 1, 1709, the king appointed as abbess Marie de Blitterswick de Moncley, sister of the bishop of Autun, soon to be promoted to the metropolitan see of Besançon. She was the same person whom Fr. Perrot had transferred from Battant and made prioress at Belmont. The saving of this convent was, unfortunately, the last success of the sorry administration of Abbot General Larcher.

The Apostasy of Nicolas Loppin

The young monk, Nicolas Loppin, cellarer since February 27, 1706, found himself in the most desperate situation during the terrible winter of 1709. There was neither wine nor wheat; he had no money and no means to feed the community, much less the poor driven to the abbey by the famine. He wrote to Paris where Larcher was active in behalf of Belmont, and asked the general for help. The abbot answered plainly that he was in no position to do anything and it was up to the cellarer to find some solution. The unfortunate monk could not face this responsibility; he took off his habit and without a word to anybody fled the monastery. He did so, however, after he had broken into the room of Dom Henriot, the abbot's secretary, and stolen everything of value he could carry away. He vanished without a trace. The disorder and confusion he left behind one may easily imagine.

Famine, Fire and the Death of Larcher

Dom Larcher came home at once, but he had to face still another embarrassing problem. For some years he failed to pay the *dimes* due the diocese of Chalon, and therefore the Chamber of Clergy seized the still available wine supply in the cellars of Vougeot. On November 29, 1709, the general was forced to sell to the mint of Dijon all silver objects he could find for the sum of 3,278 *livres*, pay the authorities of Chalon and obtain the release of the confiscated goods. Until the next harvest the bread was so bad in the abbey that those who could not digest it had to rely on help from their families.

In 1710 lightning set fire to the farmhouse of the lower court and the flames quickly spread to the nearby buildings. Larcher never recovered from the shock, although he carried on with singular determination his old lawsuit over ecclesiastical taxes, until the bishop of Chalon died on November 11, 1711. He was followed by the abbot of Cîteaux himself on March 4, 1712, in the eighty-second year of his life, after cruelly suffering from kidney-stones.

In life he was infatuated by his own dignity and high position. Among his friends he was charming, genial, and generous, but he was constantly engaged in endless lawsuits. In such matters he could rely on the expertise of his procurator general in Paris, the learned Louis Meschet, but for that reason he spent much time and money in Paris. Dom Henriot once remarked that his *fauteuil* in the Estates of Burgundy cost him so much that he could have just as well bought one of pure gold.

The Abbatial Election of 1712

As usual, the officials of Dijon under the pretext of protection, immediately sealed Petit Cîteaux, but this time the monks refused them admittance at Cîteaux and they were kept under restraint by a new royal *arrêt* issued on March 15, 1712.

After the king granted permission to proceed with the election for a new abbot, the date was set on May 19. The intervening time was spent in electioneering in which the leading local families had a full share. The king's representative was M. de La Briffe, intendant of Dijon, who carried two letters of exclusion, one for Étienne Prinstet, Roman procurator, the other for Pierre Henriot, Larcher's secretary, too closely associated with the disorders his master had left behind. Besides, the king warned the monks to elect someone young enough to be able to restore order and stability in Cîteaux.

The election, after the opening ceremonies, began as scheduled on May 19, with the participation of fifty-five professed members of the community. The first balloting brought no results. Most votes were cast for Guillaume Bouhier (21); Charles Benigne Vallot was second (14 votes), George de Maillard third (11 votes). A second round of voting was scheduled for the next morning.

Meanwhile two-thirds of the monks agreed to propose Dom Vallot for election by acclamation, but no amount of pressure was able to persuade him to accept the candidacy. Efforts were made in behalf of Dom Bouhier as well, without results. The next morning brought unexpected success to Edmond Perrot, spiritual director of the nuns of Battant, who received forty-one votes on the first ballot, in spite of his age. He was already in his seventies, a fact that Dom Bouhier was quick to point out. Perrot, however, after shedding some tears, accepted the election and the intendant raised no objections.

Perrot's First Year as Abbot of Cîteaux

Perrot accepted the see of Cîteaux but left his heart at Battant. Although the mother-house of the Order was in a deplorable condition, he made up his mind to build a church for the poor nuns in Besançon and used every opportunity to return to them. His habits remained modest. He lived in the monks' dormitory and moved to his abbatial apartment only during his last illess. He traveled mostly by public coach and took his noon meal with the monks, and on such occasions he permitted recreational conversation.

Perrot left for Paris for his royal approval only on June 15; there he was notified of the exile of Étienne Prinstet to Coetmaloën in Brittany, a victim of the party of Guillaume Bouhier and the Jesuits, who could not forgive him their defeat over Belmont. He learned in Paris that in addition to Henriot and Prinstet, the king would have prevented the election of four other monks. Perrot did everything in his power to save the ill and elderly Prinstet from exile, but all was in vain. The fine old man died a few years later.

The Marquis de La Vrillière, secretary of state, obtained a royal audience for Perrot on June 29 and his approval was issued on the same day, together with a letter for Cardinal Trémoille in Rome, urging him to promote the early issuance of the abbot's bull, which, however, he received only on March 9, 1713. He took possession of Cîteaux on March 19, an event celebrated by fireworks, an unprecedented and wasteful display of vanity. He was blessed on April 20, 1713, by the Bishop of Chalon in the episcopal chapel. In the same year he was granted the honorary title of doctor of theology at the University of Besançon; he took his oath of fidelity to the king, and on January 13, 1714, he was admitted to the Parlement of Dijon.

Hostility between himself and the Society of Jesus became manifest at his first encounter with the king's confessor, Father La Tellier. When in Versailles the Jesuit heard his name mentioned, he stepped up to him to ask if he had been Larcher's emissary at Belmont? After an affirmative answer he said: "Oh, had it been known sooner that you were to become his successor, there might have been a way to prevent it."

The Events of 1714-15

Towards the end of 1714 the Order lost Dom Louis Meschet, abbot of La Charité and procurator general in Paris, a monk of meritorious life who had contributed much to Cîteaux and the whole Order. Among other important services, he published in 1713 an excellent collection of papal privileges issued in behalf of Cistercians.[110] This work provoked the vanity of the proto-abbots who instructed a monk of Clairvaux[111] to compile another collection of documents supporting the claims of La Ferté, Pontigny, Clairvaux, and Morimond. In 1714, this was printed in Liège clandestinely, anonymously, and without the permission of the Order, under the title *Eclaircissement des privilèges de l'Ordre de Cisteaux*. This publication insured the continuation of the hostility that had existed most of the time between Cîteaux and her first four daughters.

In 1715 the famous affair of the bull *Unigenitus*[112] disturbed the tranquil disposition of the abbot of Cîteaux. Since he was assured that the papal document had been universally accepted in his Order without contradiction, he hoped that on his part a tacit approval would be sufficient. This was, however, not the case and the authorities demanded a written submission to be mailed to Father Le Tellier. The direct involvement of this Jesuit did not increase Perrot's enthusiasm, but, with some misgivings, he began to work on the complicated task. It was then that he received the news of the king's death and Le Tellier's relegation to Amiens. He threw the paper into the fire with a sigh of relief.

New Feud with the Proto-Abbots

On June 22, 1716, Perrot invited his four colleagues to Cîteaux in order to fill some vacancies among provincial vicars in France. The abbots did arrive, but before anything was done a sharp altercation broke out over the question of who should act as secretary during the consultation? Finally Perrot's point of view prevailed and the office-holders were appointed, but the proto-abbots departed firmly resolved to settle their differences with Cîteaux once and for all. They were convinced that after the death of Louis XIV and the dissolution of the committees established by him, the force of the various *arrêts* in support of Cîteaux had also been weakened, and that therefore the litigation could be resumed with better hopes for success. In December of the same year they turned to the Conseil de Conscience with an immense number of documents. What they wished to prove against Cîteaux was that in the matter of creating new officials in the absence of the General Chapter the proto-abbots had equal rights with the general, and that their authority in all other matters was the same as that of the abbot of Cîteaux.

In this context the significance of the recently published *Eclaircissement des privilèges de l'Ordre de Cisteaux* loomed very large. Therefore Perrot's advisors suggested the condemnation and proscription of this "work of darkness". After nearly two years of hesitation the general did so and in a lengthy document issued on December 10, 1716, found the book "rash, faulty in principles, distorted in meaning, tending to foster schism and disobedience in the Order", therefore he prohibited its circulation and ordered the destruction of all available copies. Unfortunately, he entrusted the execution of the decree to Dom Nicolas de Requeleine, abbot of La Charité, a house within the filiation of Clairvaux. Consequently Requeleine decided that it was safer to do practically nothing in the matter. He lived in the Parisian College of the Order and witnessed the bookbinder delivering copies of the work to Dom de Montaubon in the apartment of the abbot of Clairvaux, but he failed even to identify those involved in the propagation of the book.

Perrot's condemnation of the *Eclaircissement* was attacked immediately by Jean de Monjournal, abbot of La Ferté, and Pierre Bouchu, abbot of Clairvaux. They turned simultaneously to several courts with the charge that Perrot acted abusively in that he assumed the role of the judge in his own case and he reached beyond the limitations of his jurisdiction, i.e., beyond his own affiliation.

Perrot, on the other hand, on January 30, 1717, turned to the king with a long memorandum, asking him for the reestablishment of the committee which had been active in Cistercian litigations during Louis XIV's reign, and which would alone be responsible for all matters currently before a number of courts.

Success was faster and easier when, in the same year of 1717, Perrot asked the duke of Orleans as regent to appoint a coadjutor for the nuns of Belmont, in order to prevent the Jesuits from reaching out for that benefice on the occasion of the next vacancy.

Even the heat of the feud with the proto-abbots abated after the death on February 18, 1718, of Pierre Bouchu of

Clairvaux, the arch-enemy of Cîteaux and chief instigator of every lawsuit.

Renewed Fight Over the Right of Guardianship

The change in the royal government encouraged the officials of the bailiwick of Dijon to strengthen their position as guardians of Cîteaux at times of vacancy or General Chapter. They discovered the charter of Philippe le Bon, duke of Burgundy, issued in 1456, the only tangible basis for such a role, and attempted to interpret this old document in their favor. On August 26, 1722, the regency approved the charter of Duke Philippe, which, however, said nothing about the financial remuneration of the officials spending time at Cîteaux. Since money was the chief incentive in the matter, several officials tried to collect fees for the "services" at Cîteaux. One was the registrar (*greffier*), Turlot by name, who demanded 446 *livres* for the seventy-three days he functioned at Cîteaux during the vacancy of 1692. After a long litigation he lost the case and was compelled to pay a substantial sum for legal expenses. Similar incidents cooled the ardor of the "guardians" in future.

Dom Perrot's Ailment in 1721

In May 1721 Abbot Perrot fell to a serious malady in Besançon.[113] As his recovery became doubtful, he dictated a letter of farewell to his monks in Cîteaux. He emphasized that in building the church for the nuns of Battant he had been motivated solely by the glory of God. For the same reason, in a postscript by his own hand, he asked his successor to give time to Brother Louis l'Archer to complete some iron-works in the church of Battant. The abbot recovered, but it is difficult to absolve him for the time and expenses he spent in Besançon, while his own abbey was in dire need of both.

Visitation of the First Four Daughters of Cîteaux

Having regained his health, Abbot Perrot decided to visit

the abbeys of his four antagonists, exploiting the momentary calm following the death of Pierre Bouchu. He began his inspection at La Ferté, where he was well received and found no obstacles in discharging his duties. When he was about to leave, however, a sergeant handed him a letter of protest, declaring the visit illegal, carried out in violation of the statute of the General Chapter of 1623. The same futile ritual was carried out when he had finished his visit at Pontigny and Clairvaux, and it was only at Morimond that no appeal was made to this oft-revoked regulation.

A Catastrophic Hailstorm

In 1723 a tremendous hailstorm broke most windows of the abbey, damaged the roof, ravaged the vineyards and destroyed the still standing crops. The loss was heavy, but the monks were not forced to drink oxycrate,[114] as had been the case twelve years later in a milder emergency.

Disorders Created by the Young Generation

In 1724 the abbot was absent most of the time and since no prior had been appointed, the abbey was practically abandoned to the mercies of a group of young monks under the leadership of a graduate of the College of Saint Bernard of Paris who had brought back the loose habits of that house. His example was contagious. Unfortunately, the cellarer, trying to please them, often joined their noisy gambling parties and lost much money from the income of the abbey. This same individual is now a doctor, the prior of the abbey and provincial visitor; several members of the same group hold other high positions.

Just to give an idea of the dissipation that was going on in those years, one may refer to the debt of 18,000 *livres* in 1725, and to the expenses of 73,000 *livres* made within four years beyond the ordinary revenues of the abbey, without any significant construction or works of improvement of any kind. These same free spenders were much less enthusiastic about attending the divine services. From the end of 1724 to the end of 1726, it often occurred that no more than four monks were seated in the choir on either side.

Fire at Petit Cîteaux

God's punishing hand was not slow to strike. On the night of the 7th and 8th of October, 1726, the chimney of Petit Cîteaux in Dijon caught fire, when the only Cistercian in the house, Étienne Syrot, master of forests, was ready to sit down for his dinner. He merely instructed the servants to stoke the fireplace with wet straw, and quietly finished eating. By then the chimney was belching sparks and embers everywhere. The servants protected the roofs by spreading wet canvas on them and Dom Syrot walked into his bedroom for his well-deserved rest. By this time the houses of several neighbors were on fire and a number of frightened people were pounding on the gate of the house either for safety or for water. Dom Syrot went down only to tell the servants not to open the gate to anybody, climbed back to his room and enjoyed watching the fireworks from his window. Soon the city guard arrived on the scene, broke down the wall of the garden for access to the well, while the unperturbed Syrot could hear very well the crowd's imprecations and maledictions against himself and all other monks.

The fire was soon over but not its costly consequences, for the neighbors blamed the Cistercians for the damage they suffered. A number of lawsuits followed and eventually had to be settled by payment for the losses, totalling 7,523 *livres* in addition to legal expenses of another 1,400 *livres*.

A few days after the fire Dom Perrot came back from Besançon and, seeing the universal desolation, agreed to the appointment of a prior in the person of Dom Hugues Brun, a very capable man, formerly prior of Bonnevaux. He, however, accepted the position only on the condition that he might dismiss nine of the young troublemakers of the abbey. It was done, but in a peculiar fashion: five of them received priories, four others were transferred to other houses dependent on Cîteaux. The procurator was removed from his position and an eleventh culprit was made gatekeeper.

Problems with the Administration of the Forest

As Perrot began to experience the ebbing of his strength, he had to face another humiliating lawsuit concerning the care of the forests of Cîteaux, a responsibility of Dom Syrot. On local information the grand master of waters and forests obtained an *arrêt* from the Conseil d'État, charging illegal use and deterioration of the forests in the possession of the Order. On December 6, 1726, Cîteaux was condemned to pay the fine of 7,048 *livres*, and more was in prospect for the illegal cutting of timber. Syrot went to Paris for the defense of his administration, while Perrot protested against the *arrêt* before the controller general of finances. The affair was finally concluded in favor of Cîteaux by another *arrêt* issued by the Conseil in October 1727.

Death and Election at Cîteaux in 1727

By Christmas of 1726 the condition of Abbot Perrot had deteriorated so much that he had to be carried from his humble cell in the dormitory to the abbot's apartment. He was eighty-six years old, suffering from a variety of ailments, mainly circulatory in origin. He died in the night between January 31 and February 1, 1727. He bore his sufferings with edifying equanimity and retained his clarity of mind to his last breath. Although as administrator he was guilty of gross negligence and left behind a deplorable legacy, his personal life was impeccable: he was a model of austerity, modesty, and frugality, exemplary in religious observances. He was a man of tranquil disposition, hated lawsuits, and defended his prerogatives against the proto-abbots without enthusiasm. It was for the same reason and for his habitual absenteeism that he delegated much of his authority to his often unworthy officials.

Immediately after Perrot's death, the officials of Dijon sealed Petit Cîteaux, over the protests of Dom Vallot. On February 3 they descended on Cîteaux, fourteen persons in all, headed by the grand bailly, ready to take charge of the whole abbey, while the protesting monks turned once again to the Conseil d'État for help.

Meanwhile preparations continued for the election, to be held on April 21, in the presence of M. de La Briffe, intendant of Dijon, as royal representative. By the appointed date fifty-five electors had convened. La Briffe arrived on the eve of the election and declared that he carried a letter of exclusion for Dom George de Maillard. Upon his question concerning the most prominent candidates, the monks disclosed that they were Andoche Pernot and Bernard Antoine Bouhier, whereupon the intendant answered that he would not hesitate to vote for Pernot.

And so it happened. The next morning, after the introductory ceremonies, Andoche Pernot received on the first ballot forty-nine votes, thus becoming abbot-elect of Cîteaux. On the following day, April 22, the grand bailly and his escort left Cîteaux, fighting to the last moment over such questions as whether he was entitled to wear his sword within the walls of the abbey.

Dom Pernot soon left for Paris to obtain royal approval. Then he returned to Cîteaux, took possession of the abbey, and on November 9, was blessed with great pomp by Bishop François Madot of Chalon. The new abbot took his oath to the king only in the summer of 1728. More important, on the same occasion he obtained permission for the cutting of trees on 654 *arpens* in a reserved canton, which was to produce the income of 120,000 *livres*. As the closing act of ceremonial introduction into his office, on November 22, 1728, he was received in Dijon as "born" member of the Parlement, wearing on the occasion a glittering outfit of pontifical vestments. All this, however, could not conceal the ominous fact that he started his administration with an illegal sale of a huge quantity of timber, without the consent of his council.

———

"By this we have come to the closing of our humble narrative, leaving its continuation to our successors, if they will find the task appropriate. One should hope that they might have happier, more pleasant and more consoling things to report. It is true that what we had to tell were depressing incidents, one more so than the other. We only wish we could commit all such events to oblivion, but we set out from the beginning to record, in a just and faithful manner, all upheavals that shook the abbey of Cîteaux; therefore we could not permit ourselves to conceal the particular circumstances of important events without betraying the truth we have vowed to disclose.

"Finally, we may state without going too far, that if the abbey has somehow survived to this day, it was not for the virtue of the abbots who have governed her but as the result of the zeal and love of her children through the centuries. They have been the ones who toiled each day for her well-being, glory and honor. For this, ordinarily, they have been poorly rewarded, but never discouraged in continuing to apply all their strength for the preservation of their common mother."

APPENDIX

A LIST OF THE ABBOTS OF CÎTEAUX
From 1098 to the French Revolution

Until 1405 (Jacques II) the list follows the catalogue by J. Marilier, "Catalogue des Abbés de Cîteaux," *Cistercienser-Chronik*, 55(1948), 1-11; 63(1956), 1-6. The rest (except the last, F. Trouvé) is given according to Cotheret. For the first three centuries, by his own admission, Cotheret is not entirely reliable.

1. Robert, 1098–1099 (returned to Molesme, d. 1111).
2. Alberic, 1099–26 January 1109.
3. Stephen Harding, 1109–1133 (resigned).
4. Gui I, 1133–1134 (deposed).
5. Renard de Bar, 1134–16 December 1150.
6. Gosvin, 1151–31 March 1155.
7. Lambert, 1155–1161 (resigned).
8. Fastré, September 1161–21 April 1163.
9. Gilbert, 1163–17 October 1168.
10. Alexander, 1168–28 July 1178.
11. Guillaume I, 1178–27 November 1180.
12. Pierre I, 1180–1184 (resigned after being created bishop of Arras).
13. Bernard, 1184–1 January 1186.
14. Guillaume II, de la Prée, 1186–1189.
15. Thibaut, 1189–1190.
16. Guillaume III, 1190–3 January 1194.
17. Pierre II, 1194.

18. Gui II, de Paray, 1194–1200 (resigned after becoming a cardinal and bishop of Preneste).

19. Arnaud Amauri, 1200–12 March 1212 (resigned after becoming a cardinal and archbishop of Narbonne).

20. Arnaud II, 1212–1217 (resigned).

21. Conrad I, d'Urach, 1217–8 January 1219 (resigned after becoming a cardinal).

22. Gaucher d'Orchies, 1219–1236 (resigned).

23. Jean I, 1236–1238 (resigned).

24. Guillaume IV, de Montaigu, 1238–1243 (resigned).

25. Boniface, 1243–1258 (resigned).

26. Gui III, le Bourgoing, 1258–1262 (resigned after becoming a cardinal; d. 1272).

27. Jacques, 1262–1266 (resigned).

28. Jean II, de Ballon, 1266–9 October 1284.

29. Thibaut II, de Saulcy, 1284–2 January 1294.

30. Robert II, 1294–18 September 1294 (resigned after becoming a cardinal).

31. Rufin, 1294–30 November 1299.

32. Jean III, de Pontoise, 1299–1303 (resigned; d. 25 March 1304).

33. Henri, 1303–28 July 1315.

34. Conrad II, de Metz, 1315–6 January 1317.

35. Guillaume V, 1317–13 February 1337.

36. Jean IV, de Chaudenay, 19 February 1337–8 June 1359.

37. Jean V, le Gentil de Rougemont, 9 July 1359–23 March 1363.

38. Jean VI, de Bussières, 21 June 1363–20 December 1375 (resigned after becoming a cardinal).

39. Giraud de Bussières, 1376–9 July 1389.

40. Jacques II, de Flogny, 1389–18 April 1405.

41. Jean VII, de Martigny, 1405–21 December 1428.

42. Jean VIII, Picart, 1429 – 30 March 1440.

43. Jean IX, Vion, 1440 – 25 November 1458.

44. Gui IV, d'Autun, 1458 – 22 July 1462.

45. Himbert Martin, 1462 – 24 March 1476.

46. Jean X, de Cirey, 1476 – 20 November 1501 (resigned; d. 27 December 1503).

47. Jacques III, Theulley de Pontallier, 1501 – 25 October 1516 (resigned; d. 1 November 1516).

48. Blaise Larget d'Aisery, 1516 – 10 September 1517.

49. Guillaume VI, de Boisset, 16 September 1517 – 25 April 1521.

50. Guillaume VII, de Faucolnier, 29 April 1521 – 26 March 1540.

51. Jean XI, Loysier, 30 March 1540 – 26 December 1559.

52. Louis I, de Baissey, 6 January 1560 – 19 June 1564.

53. Jérôme de la Souchière, 1 July 1565 – 10 November 1571.

54. Nicolas I, Boucherat, 12 December 1571 – 1583 (resigned; d. 12 March 1586).

55. Edmond I, de la Croix, 13 June 1584 – 21 August 1604.

56. Nicolas II, Boucherat, 21 August 1604 – 3 May 1625.

57. Pierre III, Nivelle, 4 July 1625 – November 1635 (resigned; d. 11 February 1660).

58. Armand-Jean du Plessis, Cardinal de Richelieu, 19 November 1635 – 4 December 1642.

59. Claude Vaussin, 10 May 1645 – 1 February 1670.

60. Louis II, Loppin, 29 March 1670 – 6 May 1670.

61. Jean XII, Petit, 19 June 1670 – 15 January 1692.

62. Nicolas III, Larcher, 27 March 1692 – 4 March 1712.

63. Edmond II, Perrot, 20 May 1712 – 1 February 1727.

64. Andoche Pernot, 21 April 1727 – 14 September 1748.

65. François Trouvé, 25 November 1748 – 4 May 1791 (Cîteaux sold; d. April 26, 1797).

NOTES

1. Norgaud de Tourcy, bishop of Autun (1098-1112).
2. Hugues de Die, (c. 1040-1106).
3. See a modern edition of this *Vita* by Kolumban Spahr, *Das Leben des hl. Robert von Molesme*. Freibourg: Paulusdruckerei, 1944.
4. An obvious reference to the *Exordium parvum*, available in many editions and translations.
5. *Statuta Capitulorum Generalium Ordinis Cisterciensis.* Ed. J.-M. Canivez, 8 vols. Louvain: Bibl. de La Revue d'Histoirt Eccl., 1933-41. II, 15-16, n° 13. Henceforth: *Statuta.*
6. *Gallia Christiana in provincias ecclesiasticas distributa.* Edited by the Benedictines of Saint Maur, 16 vols. Paris, 1715-1765.
7. . . . *quamdiu vos et successores vestri in ea, quam nunc observatis, frugalitatis et observantiae disciplina permanseritis.*
8. *Collecta quorundam privilegiorum Ordinis Cisterciensis.* Dijon: Mettlinger, 1491. (The date given here by Cotheret is erroneous.)
9. I.e., *Exordium parvum.*
10. Correctly: *Bibliotheca Patrum Cisterciensium.* Ed. Bertrandus Tissier.
11. Edited by Julien Paris, abbot of Foucarmont.
12. See this question discussed in detail by L. J. Lekai, 'Nicolas Cotheret and the Conditional Nature of the "Privilegium Romanum",' *Cîteaux*, 31(1980), 1-7.
13. Angelus Manrique, *Annales Cistercienses.* 4 vols. Lugduni, 1642.
14. See its critical edition by Bruno Griesser, Roma: Editiones Cistercienses, 1961.
15. Better known as Robert of Torigny, abbot of Mont-Saint-Michel, author of a *Tractatus de immutationibus ordinis monachorum.* Ed. L. Delisle (Rouen, 1873). Also in Migne, PL 202:1309ff.
16. *Statuta*, I, 45, n° 1.
17. This must be the bull of Feb. 2, 1165, issued in Sens, and edited by J. Marilier, *Chartes et documents concernant l'abbaye de Cîteaux, 1098-1182.* Roma: Editiones Cistercienses, 1961, pp. 140-142. Henceforth: Marilier, *Chartes.*
18. The identity of this brief remains uncertain. It is missing from Marlier, *Chartes.*
19. Claude Fleury (1640-1723), popular church-historian and private tutor in the court of Louis XIV.
20. *Statuta*, I, 75-76 gives a different version of the affair. Cotheret borrows from Jean de Cirey's much later work, *Dialogus de prospero et adverso statu ordinis* . . . still in MS.

21. Thirteenth-century chronicler, monk of Saint Denis.

22. See on him a long serial by Gregor Müller, 'Der hl. Petrus, Erzbischof von Tarantaise', *Cistercienser-Chronik*, 3(1891).

23. Marilier, *Chartes*, pp. 198-203.

24. *Statuta*, I, 180, nº 55.

25. For most dry products 1 *setier*=156.10 liters.

26. Alonso Chacón (1540-1599), Spanish Dominican, author of a history of popes.

27. Ferdinando Ughelli (1595-1670), famous Cistercian author of the monumental *Italia Sacra* in 9 vols. (1643-1648).

28. François Eudes de Mézeray (1610-1683), author of a voluminous *Histoire de la France* (1643-1651) of great reputation.

29. Louis Moreri (1643-1680), French scholar, author of the *Grand dictionnaire historique* (1674).

30. *Statuta*, I, 311, nº 18.

31. Great historian of the thirteenth century. His *Chronica maiora* was edited by H. R. Luard in the Rolls Series, nº 57, London, 1883.

32. This visit features prominently in *Statuta*, II, 274-276, nos. 4-13.

33. See his short biography in the *Dictionary of National Biography*. Oxford: Clarendon Press, 1950, XI, 1083.

34. See for all references to the Parisian College the *Index* volume of *Statuta*, under Sancti Bernardi Collegium Parisiense.

35. This is under 1261 in *Statuta*, II, 477, nº 9.

36. Cotheret borrowed the whole material for this subject from J. Paris, *Nomasticon Cisterciense*, Paris, 1670, pp. 371-464. Unfortunately, this is missing from the Séjalon edition of the *Nomasticon* (Solesmes, 1892).

37. Nicolas.

38. Étienne.

39. Geoffrroy de Beaulieu.

40. Guy de Rochefort (1250-1266).

41. This work, still in MS, is attributed to Jean de Cirey, abbot of Cîteaux (1476-1501).

42. *Statuta*, III, 69, nº 8.

43. Jacques Bouillart (d. 1726), Maurist historian, author of *Histoire de l'abbaye royale de Saint-Germain-des-Prés*, in fol. Paris, 1724.

44. Jacques Dubreuil, *Chronicon abbatum regalis monasterii S. Germani a Pratis*, in fol. Paris, 1603. The author was a monk of the same abbey.

45. Pierre Dupuy (1582-1651), noted French historian. The work here referred to is *Histoire du différend entre le pape Boniface VIII et le roy Philippe le Bel* (1655).

46. Adrien Baillet (1649-1706), *Histoire des démêlés . . .* (Paris, 1717).

47. There is nothing more known about this MS, which was obviously in the library of Cîteaux in the eighteenth century.

48. See this Constitution, known as *Fulgens sicut stella* or 'Benedictina' in *Statuta*, III, 410-436.

49. This edition was initiated by Dom Sainte-Marthe in 1715.

50. The MS was certainly in the library of Cîteaux and was inspired by Jean de Cirey.

51. There are three known copies of this MS: Grand Séminaire of Bruges; Altenberg near Cologne; Arsenal in Paris.

52. Ferry de Grancey (1415-1436).

53. Hugues d'Orges (1416-1431).

54. *Statuta*, IV, 427, n° 38.

55. Henri d'Avaugour (1421-1446).

56. Philippe de Lévis (1425-1454).

57. Cardinal Jean Rollin (1436-1483). See the whole story in G. D. Mansi, *Sacrorum conciliorum nova et amplissima collectio*, (Florence & Venice, 1759-1798), XXX, 1221-1223.

58. *Statuta*, V, 317-319, n° 7.

59. From here to the end of the century the narrative is borrowed from the memoirs of Jean de Cirey, no longer in existence.

60. Filippo Calandrini (1448-1476).

61. Jean Rollin.

62. Jean de Poupet (1461-1480).

63. This MS (perhaps even printed work) does not seem to have survived.

64. *Statuta*, V, 445-447, n° 52.

65. *Statuta*, V, 454-457, nos. 16-17.

66. *Statuta*, V, 481-483, n° 37.

67. Correctly: Jean III de Bourbon.

68. *Statuta*, V, 607-608, n° 79.

69. See note n° 8.

70. See note n° 20. The copy preserved in the Archives Départementales in Dijon is of 185 pages on paper, therefore hardly can be the 'original' as the printed catalogue asserts.

71. See note n° 50.

72. See the text in *Statuta*, VI, 87-97.

73. Pierre Palliot, *Le Parlement de Bourgogne*. Dijon, 1649.

74. Plot of land which a man could cultivate in a day.

75. Plot of meadow a mower could clear in a day.

76. A square of about 220 feet on each side.

77. About 358 liters.

78. Over 400 square meters, or territory a worker could cultivate in a day.

79. Cotheret gives the long story of the feud between the two observances on the basis of some of the printed pamphlets published by both sides. The largest collection of such pamphlets is in Bibliothèque Nationale, Paris, under Ld[17]. See the whole question detailed by Louis J. Lekai, *The Rise of the Cistercian Strict Observance*. Washington: Cath. Univ. of America Press, 1968.

80. Cotheret's low opinion of this work is justifiable. It is a mere compilation by Hippolyte Hélyot (1660-1716) of undeserved popularity. It covers this subject biased in favor of the Reform with many factual errors.

81. Sébastien Zamet (1615-1655).

82. Jacques de Neuchèze (1624-1658).

83. Cotheret's extremely dark portrait of Nivelle must be read with reservations. He had many enemies both before and after his election, not only the popular Charles Boucherat, but also the very influential Bishop Zamet and Cardinal La Rochefoucauld, together with the whole circle of Port-Royal. Among the many damaging pamphlets and gossips it was certainly difficult to separate truth from fable.

84. This last statement is certainly erroneous. There was no Cistercian convent in Meaux. The third women's house breaking away from Cîteaux was Tart, but the whole movement was the work of Zamet, who wanted to form out of these communities a new order under his leadership, the 'Daughters of the Blessed Sacrament', without success, however.

85. François de Verthamon.

86. Louis Dinet (1621-1650).

87. See the voluminous MS which includes Vaussin's first trip to Rome, in Bibliothèque Municipale de Dijon, MSS 2683, 2684, amounting altogether to 943 pages. It is a modern copy.

88. This was the source of Hélyot's (see note n° 80) story and of the even more influential A.-F. Gervaise, *Histoire générale de la réforme de l'Ordre de Cisteaux en France* (1746). These two works dominated scholarly opinion until the 1960s.

89. The reason of inaction was the 'Corsican Guard affair' of Aug. 20, 1662, when this papal guard clashed with the escort of the French ambassador in Rome. The incident had grave diplomatic consequences.

90. The student was Joseph Montulé of the reformed Perseigne, and the incident created a hostile atmosphere in Rome against the Reform. Montulé, instead of reprimand, received the priory of Melleray.

91. Vaussin left France in a papal galleon in the company of Cardinal Chigi and arrived at Rome on October 9. He left the city early in March, 1665 and arrived at Cîteaux a few days after April 15. See the details of this phase of the Roman negotiations in my book, *The Rise of the Cistercian Strict Observance*, pp. 119-131.

92. See its full text (*In suprema . . .*) in *Statuta*, VII, 426-440.

93. See the records of the Chapter in *Statuta*, VII, 438-466.

94. George Bourée, member of an old bourgeois family of Dijon.

95. François-Pierre Mary (1666-1696).

96. Abbot of Prières since 1630; died on June 2, 1673.

97. It was immediately printed and widely distributed in Paris.

See one of the many surviving copies in Bibliothèque Nationale, MS Fr. 10,565, fols. 238-241.

98. François de Harley de Champvallon (1661-1695).

99. See the list of all available printed pamphlets covering this matter published in *Analecta Cisterciensia*, 25(1969), 107-128.

100. Charles Colbert, marquis de Croissy, foreign secretary since 1679, brother of the 'Grand Colbert'.

101. César Cardinal d'Estrées (1628-1714), bishop of Laon, special envoy in Rome negotiating in the *régale* affair.

102. 'War of the League of Augsberg', 1688-1697.

103. Henri Felix de Tassi (1687-1711). See a pamphlet in this matter published by the bishop, in Bibliothèque Nationale, Ld[17] 92.

104. François de Clermont-Tonnerre (1661-1701).

105. See fifteen printed pamphlets on this and related issues in Bibl. Nat., Ld[17] 112-123.

106. See thirteen printed pamphlets on this famous debate in Bibl. Nat., Ld[17] 98-109.

107. Louise-Hollandine, daughter of Elector Frederick V of the Palatinate.

108. Benôit-Henri Duchesne (1684-1703).

109. This is the story that seems to prove that in 1702 Cotheret himself was a student at the College.

110. *Privilèges de l'Ordre de Cisteaux*, a book of 535 pages and to this day the best collection of papal documents.

111. Richard Montaubon, secretary of the abbot of Clairvaux. His work is of 494 pages.

112. Issued by Clement XI in 1713, the bull was intended to terminate the Jansenist controversy.

113. It was not an illness (as Cotheret seems to believe), but a coach-accident, resulting in a nearly fatal head-injury. See for details G. Müller, 'Aus Cîteaux in den Jahren 1717-1744', *Cistercienser-Chronik*, 12(1900), 56-58.

114. A mixture of water and vinegar.

CISTERCIAN PUBLICATIONS INC.

TITLES LISTING

THE CISTERCIAN FATHERS SERIES

THE CISTERCIAN STUDIES SERIES

Temporarily out of print   †Forthcoming